HEART OF THE RAINCOAST

Queen Charlotte Strait. (Photo by Alexandra Morton)

HEART OF THE RAINCOAST
A LIFE STORY

ALEXANDRA MORTON AND BILLY PROCTOR

First TouchWood Edition 2004
Reprinted 2009
(Originally published by Horsdal & Schubart Publishers Ltd.
under ISBN 0-920663-61-3 in 1998; reprinted in 1999 and 2001)

TouchWood Editions
www.touchwoodeditions.com

Library and Archives Canada Cataloguing in Publication
Morton, Alexandra, 1957–
Heart of the raincoast : a life story/Alexandra Morton and Billy Proctor.

ISBN 978-1-894898-26-3

1. Proctor, Billy, 1934–   2. Pacific Coast (B.C.) — Biography. 3. Pacific Coast
(B.C. — Description and travel. I. Proctor, Billy, 1934–   II. Title.

FC3845.P2Z49 2004   971.1'104'092   C2004-903997-0

Front-cover photograph: *Ocean Dawn* in Knight Inlet, by Alexandra Morton.
Back-cover photographs: Billy Proctor, by Alexandra Morton;
Alexandra Morton, by Jarret Morton.
Maps and drawings: Alexandra Morton.
All poetry: Jae Proctor.

TouchWood Editions acknowledges the financial support for its publishing program
from the Government of Canada through the Book Publishing Industry Development
Program (BPIDP), Canada Council for the Arts, and the province of British Columbia
through the British Columbia Arts Council and the Book Publishing Tax Credit.

The interior pages of this book have been printed on 100 % post-consumer recycled
paper, processed chlorine free, and printed with vegetable-based inks.

PRINTED IN CANADA

DEDICATIONS

To Mum. *Billy Proctor*

To the whales that led me into the Mainland, and their return one day soon. *Alexandra Morton*

Introduction

THERE ARE THREE voices in this book. The poetry is Jae Proctor's and has been edited from her diaries. The inset sections are by her son, Billy Proctor, and the rest is told by me, Alexandra Morton, a neighbour. The story is based on conversations with the Proctors and other people of the Broughton Archipelago, locally known as the "Mainland."

The Mainland is what people call the area between and including Drury Inlet and Knight Inlet. Much of the Mainland is actually made up of islands, but it is all lumped together under the one term. It is an archipelago of untamed beauty, and within its protected waters life teems and thrives. People who live in these islands are known as "Mainlanders."

I came to the Mainland following whales. I am a whale researcher. I did not expect to find people in the wilderness I chose for my research. My days among whales provoked many questions and I realized that to understand killer whales, I had to learn about salmon. I found many clues as to why whales do what they do by listening to Billy Proctor. His knowledge was in many ways my Rosetta Stone, the translation I needed to make sense of whale movements.

During the 15 years I have known Billy, I have watched an extraordinary process. Born in a time and place where bounties were paid on every predator, from crows to cougars, this man, who never went to school, has become a spokesman for common sense in a world gone mad.

Billy spent his life becoming one of the most successful people in the Mainland. When he reached his fifties, and could have begun to relax, he was struck out of the blue with self-imposed questions about the impact of his work.

It all caught up to him one day in the Burdwood Islands. He was handlogging a beautiful fir, doing what he loved. He was a highliner fisherman, had one of the biggest handlogging quotas on the coast, a good trapline, a boat ways, a sawmill and the biggest homestead for miles around, but what had his success done to him, his family and his home? He sat on the fresh stump all that afternoon and thought and thought and thought. And then he decided it must be time to put something back.

Deeply shy and self-effacing, Billy was led by these questions to shoulder the responsibility of negotiating on behalf of the natural world he understands so well. Public speaking terrified him, but he realized it was speak up or watch his homeland die.

Today, he has met with all levels of government, offering the wealth of his knowledge. At meetings stacked high with papers, graphs and projected outcomes, Billy's words blow through in a gale of truth. While he has observed everything from periwinkle migrations to bears, his greatest contribution is his understanding of salmon, the lifeblood of this coast.

Salmon have become a political nightmare because their life cycle requires habitat from the headwaters of British Columbia's mountains to the open waters of the Pacific. Provincial, federal and international governments are brought into contentious contact over salmon. While some industries and levels of government might like to see wild salmon quietly slip away, people love the fish instinctively and passionately. Politicians arc pulled by the conflicting demands of hydro companies, oil companies, developers, sport and commercial fishermen and preservationists, until the fish themselves have been reduced to return probabilities, pieces, dollars and cents.

The biggest trouble with managing fish is their lack of visibility; no one can see them. When they fail to appear in their rivers, no one leas any idea what happened to them. Did they die at sea, or at the mouths of their streams? Did a sport fisherman kill the last member of a specific run or was it a driftnet? Was it poisoned by a pesticide, infected with an exotic fish-firm disease, or eaten by a mackerel? I have noticed that whenever salmon arc discussed, emotions run high and no one wants to be responsible for their demise.

After a lifetime of observing, hunting and raising salmon, Billy knows the fish as do only a few others on this coast and he has reluctantly decided to do what he can to ensure that the children of the future have the opportunity to live On a planet where salmon thrive. This is his story.

Alexandra Morton

Update

The survival of both orcas and wild salmon is in doubt. Since this book was published in 1998, Billy and I have seen the salmon-farming industry grow at a ruthless pace — bigger farms, more sites and plans to expand upcoast into some of the largest salmon-producing waters in British Columbia. When fishing-lodge owner Chris Bennett brought me two tiny new salmon covered in sea lice, my life changed direction. Sea lice flourish on salmon farms, and everywhere the farms share water with wild salmon, the wild salmon collapse. Sea lice on baby salmon are considered the cause.

So I now study sea lice. Government and industry are aligned against me — there is no more Ministry of Environment under the current government, so there is less provincial protection for the natural world — but Billy taught me that fish *do* talk if you listen and look hard enough. I can be found most days staring into the water ... I am measuring an extinction, but I do not plan to allow these fish to pass quietly.

As lice-infested baby salmon twinkle to the sea floor like a constellation of falling stars, Billy and I both know that rage will not help them. Read this book and learn about a lifetime spent studying the rhythms of life. Salmon are sacred, a gift to us that we are entrusted to pass on to those not yet born. In another place, Billy would have been a scientist, his ability to see and record are so acute. The only act that can save the salmon and indeed ourselves is the simple passing on of knowledge.

The fledgling threads of alliances for change have continued to thrive. With the Internet connection, when fishermen bring me strange parasites on the fish they catch in front of salmon farms, I can send the pictures out to the world, and the alliance for life grows stronger.

We humans have become the greatest renewable energy source on Earth: what we love thrives; what we disregard withers. This gives each of us control over the fate of the planet.

Next to love, humanity's most important energy is money, so we must be thoughtful about where we apply it. When we buy something, we fuel the system behind it. When you buy a local food, you support your community; when you buy corporate items, you may be supporting the clearing of a tropical forest. Rather than seeing ourselves as powerless, we must realize that we *are* the power.

Alexandra Morton, 2004

I have fished from the tide rips of Blackfish Sound to the shoals of Rennel Sound. I have fished from Cape Cook in the south to Langara Light in the north. I have weathered a storm off Cape Scott where the screaming southeasters blow. I have sat out a hurricane in Sea Otter Cove when you could not stand on deck. I have also crossed from Cape St. James to Pine Island on a beautiful moonlit night with just a gentle rolling sea.

I have seen the sunrise on the ocean on many a summer morn. I have also seen the most beautiful sunsets on the sea. A burst of flame and not one the same.

I have seen it when there was a sockeye on every hook with the checkers overflowing. I have also seen it when no matter what I did, it always seemed to be wrong. From dawn till dark we ply our trade out where the ocean storms are made. We plow around in a hell's half-acre on the edge of the old grey widow-maker. With hook-scarred fingers we bitch and complain, but I am sure we will stay to the bitter end.

Top Knot, Shag Rock, Seven Mile, Dropoff, Cash Creek, Goose Bay, Ramsy Spot, Yankee Spot, Glory Hole, Two Peaks, Pine Island, Cape Cook, Horseshoe Grounds. These are all places trollers know, just to name a few. In all kinds of weather you will see the trollers' poles go waving by, etched sharp against a lead-grey sky. I have seen a lot of changes in my time. I have seen a lot of good years and I have seen a few bad years. If I had to do it all again, I am sure I would do it the same.

Billy Proctor

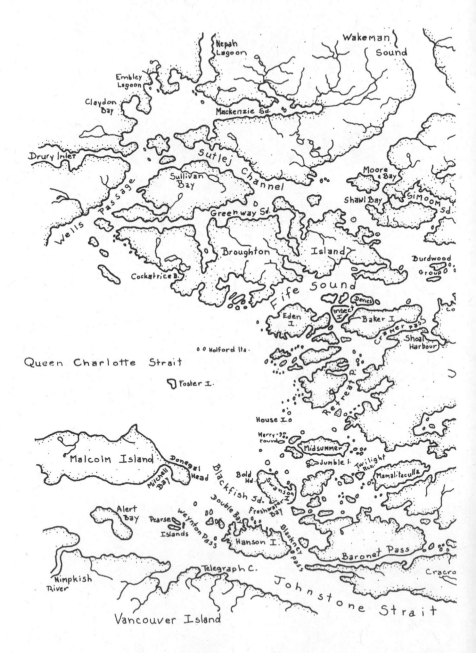

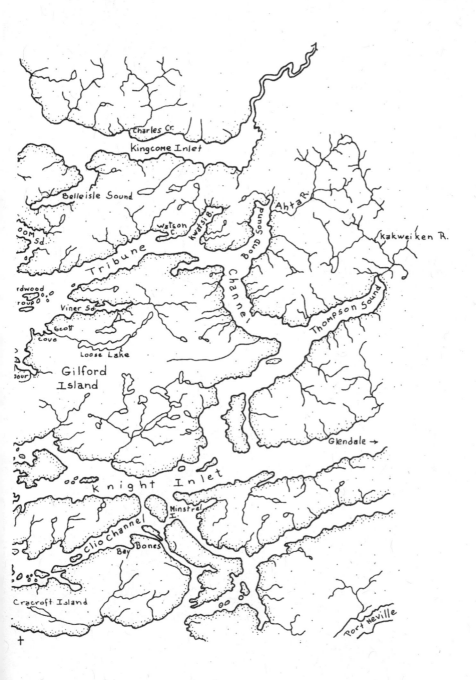

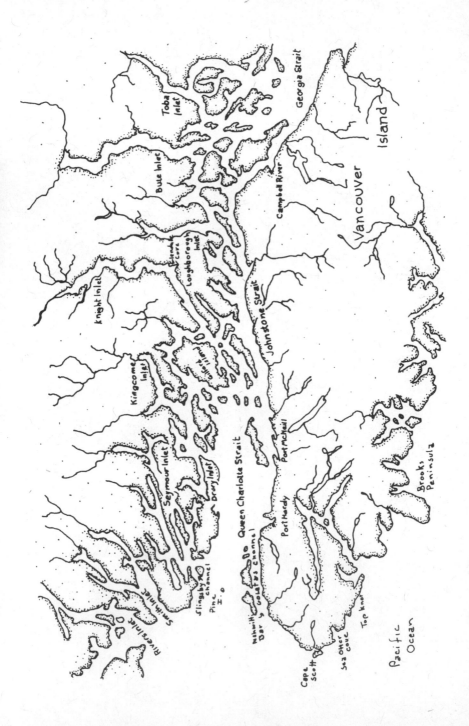

Toba Inlet
Georgia Strait
Vancouver Island
Bute Inlet
Campbell River
Loughborough Inlet
Knight Inlet
Johnstone Strait
Kingcome Inlet
Seymour Inlet
Drury Inlet
Queen Charlotte Strait
Port McNeill
Port Hardy
Brooks Peninsula
Slingsby Channel
Pine Channel
Smith Inlet
Rivers Inlet
Goletas Channel
Cape Scott
Sea Otter Cove
Top knot
Pacific Ocean

CHAPTER ONE

I see your kind and cheery face
Wishing you were here taking my place.
You would know just what to do
And I wouldn't be so lonely and blue.

THE SNOW ON the central coast of British Columbia was unusually deep the winter of 1942. Normally dark green, the hillsides were white, the trees bent under the weight of wet snow. Sharp cracks reverberated as ancient hemlocks, firs and cedars broke the snowy silence and fell deep in the forests. On a cold February morning, a sturdy Scottish woman, her floral print dress peeking out from beneath a long wool coat, pulled her socks up over her shoes to keep her from slipping and continued hacking at an old float-log, peeling away the bark.

The float was 60 big logs lashed together and it carried an A-frame. Reaching 100 feet high and rigged for logging with pulleys, cables and a winch, the A-frame was an essential piece of logging equipment. But this winter it served another purpose; it was a source of heat. Each low tide brought the float to rest on the beach where the woman could reach it. Unable to cut logs, she was harvesting bark to burn in her stove. The massive fir float-logs were tightly clad in thick, energy-rich bark laced with pungent sap. This kind of bark produced hot, slow-burning, life-sustaining embers.

As the woman attacked the logs with grim determination, a slim wisp of a boy quickly gathered them up. At seven years old, he couldn't swing the axe effectively, but his mum was grateful for what assistance he could offer. They worked fast to fill the wheel-barrow before the returning tide took the logs out of reach for another 12 hours. Fir trees don't part easily with their bark and this one was encrusted with sharp-edged barnacles and dripping mussels. Each load provided a few hours of warmth for the mother and son, alone on their island with no firewood. Their trim little house was not insulated and already the waterlines had frozen solid.

The A-frame at Freshwater Bay, Swanson Island, from which Jae and Billy chipped bark.
(PHOTO BY JAE PROCTOR)

Three weeks earlier, on February 5, 1942, Bill Proctor had departed in his boat on a routine mail run to Alert Bay. The Proctors ran the post office out of their home in Freshwater Bay and it was up to Bill to bring the mail sacks across Blackfish Sound twice a week. He liked the trips to town and was never much bothered by the restless, often violent body of water he had to cross.

Blackfish Sound is open to both of the dominant winds of this coast. Whether it's a southeast wind howling up Johnstone Strait or a northwester whistling down Queen Charlotte Strait, Blackfish Sound gets excited. Her narrow passages to the south, Blackney and Weyton, bottleneck the power of the flood tide. A big incoming tide, flooding from the Pacific Ocean, raises the sea level as much as 17 feet. When forced through narrow passages, its power erupts into huge whirlpools and slick boils. If wind and tide flow together they calm the surface, but when they run against each other, huge waves stand straight up, tossing anything riding upon them.

Bill had shared a beer with the boys that night before heading home. It was 11:00 PM when he went down to the boat and the night was black with rain, wind and roaring waves. His friends told him to wait a few hours, until dawn, but Bill was one of those who are confident beyond doubt. He knew what his boat could take, he knew this stretch of water and he had seen it worse. There was no reason not to go. But shortly after leaving, Bill must have encountered something unexpected, something he hadn't figured on, and that cost him his life. Very possibly the boat simply took an unexpected wave while he was on deck. Sometimes the smallest miscalculations cause lifelong ripples of disruption and sorrow.

Young Billy usually accompanied his father on these mail runs, but this time fate had the boy stay home. In the morning, the empty space where his dad tied the boat silently declared trouble. Billy rowed out to a small island on the edge of their bay, called Flower Island, for a clear view of Blackfish Sound. The water lay docile now, as if the storm had never occurred, and the boy tried to pull the image of his father's boat out of the grey of the far side.

What he didn't know was that the 32-foot gillnetter had already been found that morning. Named *Zev*, she had thrown her skipper

Billy at Freshwater Bay, Flower Island to the right. (PHOTO BY JAE PROCTOR)

and survived the night without him. The sea gave up Bill's body three weeks later. Toots Hinton of Alert Bay discovered it among the driftwood at the high-tide mark on a beach near where *Zev* had been found.

Filled with the fear of not knowing, the boy kept watch for three days on the little island and finally a boat did appear on the horizon. As it plied a course straight towards the Proctor homestead, Billy could see it wasn't *Zev* long before it entered the bay. It was the police boat, carrying the terrible news.

That is how Jae Proctor found herself alone on Swanson Island, a widow with a young child. She had only a rowboat, no means of communication and no immediate neighbours. Given these circumstances, her friends thought she would move away, allow the rainforest to reclaim the homestead, and pull the comforts of civilization around herself. But Jae chose not to abandon the life she had built with her husband and if she had any doubts, she never mentioned them to her son.

★★★

4

Janet married Bill Proctor in 1924 in Vancouver. Bill owned a pile driver and following the wedding he headed up the coast alone to Charles Creek, in magnificent Kingcome Inlet. Charles Creek was once the site of a big native village which was destroyed years before Europeans came to the coast, by a massive landslide. The creek was also home to large runs of coho.

In 1906, a man named Hicky built a cannery at Charles Creek, called it Hicky Fisheries, and ran it for about 18 years. Hicky rented boats and nets to fishermen and in return they had to sell their catch to him. Hicky owned the fishing rights to Kingcome Inlet and Wakeman Sound. All species of salmon spawned in the big Wakeman and Kingcome rivers. Hicky's fishermen were not allowed west of the Bradley Point-Philips Point boundary at the mouth of the inlet.

In 1910 Otto Schone travelled to Charles Creek, looking for a trapline. He liked what he saw, purchased the trapping rights and built a house on the bank of the creek near the beach. He built seven small cabins back in the valley to stay in as he worked his trapline.

Hicky's cannery prospered. He virtually owned the rich waters of Kingcome Inlet and because he decided what to pay "his" fishermen he became a wealthy man. Eventually, Hicky sold out to another man, Stumpf, who renamed the cannery Kingcome Packers. Stumpf's fishermen could fish anywhere, but they had to sell to him. The cannery burned in 1924 and that was when Bill Proctor was hired to rebuild it.

It took Bill a full year to get the cannery back into operation. Its remoteness caused countless delays while he waited for supplies. When Charles Creek became liveable again, Bill sent for his wife. Janet Proctor's trip north to join her husband was her first journey up the coast. She boarded the 50-foot *Cheyney*, built for Kingcome Packers in 1925 to run supplies from Vancouver to Charles Creek.

The trip went smoothly through the passages east of Vancouver Island, past many small floating communities along the way. The shoreline slipped by in shades of grey, and cold rain fell without stop. Halfway up Johnstone Strait a southeaster hit. The wind was

5

behind them for most of the day, but just before dark, when their course forced them to turn broadside to the wind, it built to storm force. With only a two cylinder Atlas engine, the packer was under-powered and the snowy gale proved the stronger force. When the boat stopped making headway, the skipper decided to spend the night in the protection of Scott Cove on Gilford Island. There, with the wind moaning in the rigging, Jae tucked into her dinner, a can of pork and beans. It was Christmas Eve.

On Christmas Day *Cheyney* continued her run north and when the boat turned into Kingcome Inlet, civilization fell away to a memory. The broad expanse of water danced under the breeze, and a brilliant glacier radiated ageless cold far above. The effect was dazzling. Jae had considered *Cheyney* a large boat at the crowded Vancouver dock but now, in the immensity of the inlet, it shrank. Jae had never felt quite so small.

When *Cheyney* turned into Charles Creek another emotion hit. Jae was appalled. Somehow Bill's letters had failed to prepare her for her new home, a 10- by 12-foot shack perched on an old scow. Jae had been raised in Alberta in the elegant comfort of a grand home and she did not consider this pile of boards fit to live in. It

Bill Proctor at Charles Creek, in his dugout canoe. (PHOTO BY JAE PROCTOR)

wasn't even on land. After two miserable months, she couldn't stand it and despite her strong affection for her handsome man, Jae fled back to Vancouver.

That was Jae Proctor's last retreat. Come spring, she decided to return to her husband and Kingcome Inlet, and this time Bill wisely moved her ashore into a company house. In time, the cannery felt like home. Charles Creek has the advantage of being on the sunny side of the inlet. While the dark side is frosted by the glacier, the sun warmed Jae's home and she planted a few flowers. In the spring, glacial meltwater coloured the water a pale milky green, and nothing could surpass the sight of whales surfing the tumble of diamond-capped waves in a brisk summer westerly.

In 1927, Stumpf, the cannery owner, hired Bill to build another cannery in Leroy Bay, Smith Inlet, and Jae went with him. The biggest job was digging and blasting a 500-foot tunnel through a hill to bring fresh water to the cannery. Canneries required large amounts of water and Stumpf wasn't going to let a hill stand in the way of progress.

Jae was becoming accustomed to the coast and she enjoyed Leroy Bay from the start. Stumpf had a 22-foot open boat, *Sardine*, that Jae could use whenever she wanted, and she liked to take it out, though she never learned to start its four hp Easthope. She always got Bill to start it and just hoped the motor wouldn't stall while she was out. Being an Easthope, it never did. When the cannery was finished, the Proctors went back to Charles Creek to camp watch for the winter. A Japanese crew at the cannery was kept busy building gillnets, tying up to 10,000 meshes a day, and Jae took a job loading needles with twine for these net men.

In 1928 Bill and Jae decided to go fishing with Stumpf's gillnet fleet. Stumpf wintered his fishing skiffs at Charles Creek and towed them north to Smith Inlet each spring. The first week of June, Jae boarded the Kingcome Company packer, *Saugeen*. "Their" skiff was on the towline with 19 others, packed with all their belongings. *Saugeen* headed out for open water like a mother merganser, her brood of the little skiffs bobbing behind her.

The coast from Vancouver to Alaska is called the "Inside Passage," but there are a few places where the ocean swells roll

Fishboats at Charles Creek, 1929. (PHOTO BY JAE PROCTOR)

straight in and it is not "inside" at all. Offshore winds build these swells until they tower over small boats. When the west wind meets one of the strongest tidal currents in the world, in Nakwakto Rapids, Slingsby Channel, trouble can brew.

The trip north to Smith Inlet was beautiful. Jae saw Gray whales and humpbacks feeding along the wide beaches south of Cape Caution. Dall's porpoise rode the bow wave in flashes of black and white like tiny killer whales. With no responsibilities, Jae spent her days relaxing. However, that run north brought disaster. A westerly had been blowing for several days, pushing the waves to a formidable size. The skipper of *Saugeen* was more concerned about making good time than about safety and he foolishly cut straight across the entrance of Slingsby Channel during a big June ebb tide.

Slingsby drains Seymour and Belize inlets and this tide was dropping 17 feet, with billions of gallons of water fighting to get out through the narrow channel. The force is so great that the island in the middle of the rapids actually trembles during these big tides. When the westerly swell collided with this river of water racing to escape, the sea reared into a fury of huge "haystacks," 10 to 15 feet high. Giant pyramids rose and fell away beneath the boat, seething with brute power. While *Saugeen* pitched and rolled hugely through the haystacks, her weight kept her from rolling too far to one side.

The little skiffs, however, danced madly. Like wild colts they reared and bolted against the towline, smashed downwards, bucked and tipped off the sides of the waves. Half the miniature fleet dipped their gunwales beneath the violent water and rolled over. One of the skiffs that went down was the Proctors', with all their summer gear. When their boat flipped, Jae lost her most precious possession, her camera.

Today, it is very expensive to become a commercial fisherman. A boat and salmon licence cost well over $100,000. In the 1920s it was much simpler. Kingcome Packers supplied the boat and nets: the big investment was endurance.

Cannery boats were spartan little vessels, 32 feet long with flat bottoms, no mast and only oars for propulsion. Hundreds of these skiffs were built out of six shiplapped cedar planks and painted "cannery red." Names were never bestowed upon these little boats, only numbers, and conditions on board were primitive at best. The only protection the Proctors had from rain and wind was a piece of six-foot-square canvas they secured across the bow in bad weather.

During the day Bill generally rolled the tarp back to give them more room to "pick" the nets. On today's gillnetters a large drum spools the net aboard, but in those days fishermen pulled the nets into the boat by hand. The nets had to be picked every few hours to harvest the salmon and clean off debris. Even on sunny days, nothing stayed dry in the little boat. The struggling fish threw water, slime, jellyfish bits and seaweed everywhere. Ocean spray dampened everything, encrusting people and supplies in a layer of salt and of course, it rained frequently.

Jae cooked simple meals on a little primus stove. Bacon and eggs and lots of thick, hearty stews were regular fare. On the top of the stove she rigged a four-gallon can as an oven. The warm, sweet smell of baking cookies cut through the odour of fish and soggy wool like a little bit of heaven.

Kingcome Packers supplied the Proctors with two nets, a five-inch mesh for sockeye and a 6½-inch mesh for coho. Today's nets come in every shade of blue-green imaginable, making them invisible to salmon under different conditions. With space-age names such as Super Star 39 and Mono 2,000, they are made in a wide range of mesh sizes and the strands are as light as gossamer.

The Proctors' nets were white linen and very heavy. While the thick linen fibres were easier on fishermen's fingers than today's fine synthetics, they were much easier for salmon to see and avoid. Cedar buoys were used to float the nets and lead weights attached to the bottom pulled them taut. The nets were the same length as today, 1,200 feet.

Every Sunday, from the beginning of June through November, Jae sat in the little skiff with her husband as the packer towed them out to fish the inlet. The packer pulled ten skiffs at a time on a heavy line. As they passed the spot Bill wanted to fish, he released the bow line. This swung his skiff's bow outward, away from any boats behind them; then Jae let the stern line go and they were on their own.

As today, fishing openings began at 6:00 PM, marked by a loud blast. At first it seemed strange to Jae and Bill to start anything so late in the day, but sunset is the prime time to have a gillnet in the water, because fish hit most heavily at dusk. The low angle of light on the water must somehow make it difficult for them to

Cannery boats, Charles Creek, Kingcome Inlet, 1928. (PHOTO BY JAE PROCTOR)

10

see the net. Without the sounders and airplanes used today to find fish, knowing where to set was difficult. Bill and Jae soon learned to read the water.

Fish are traditionalists, following the same ancient routes discovered by their ancestors thousands of years ago. These "fish highways" are currents. Unlike terrestrial pathways, fish highways snake and undulate in response to the strength of each tide, the amount of fresh water pouring out of the rivers, the wind, even the tilt of the planet. Salmon ride these currents, storing their precious energy for the arduous trip up rivers to spawn. As they approach their rivers, salmon hitch a ride on each flood tide, then rest in protected spots during the ebb.

When water pouring out of an inlet meets the incoming tide, the two currents slide under and over and along each other. Everything from larval marine organisms to logs and fish is trapped in these tidal embraces and this is where salmon school, feeding voraciously. While this is the best place to catch fish, the tangle of debris which collects makes a terrible mess of a net. Sticks, seaweed, logs and huge roots are all caught, along with the fish.

Gillnetting takes as much skill as any other form of fishing and the fledgling fisherman has to gradually piece together a plan. Even if thousands of fish pass beneath a boat, just throwing a net in the water won't catch them. After a period of experimentation the Proctors decided that Jae would row while Bill fed the tightly knotted linen into the water. Bill made certain there were no twists or tangles and Jae gave the net its shape. As Bill threw out the first cork Jae began a semi-circle, then she rowed in a straight line until the end when she made another curve.

When salmon approach a gillnet, a few might run blindly into the net and slide through until the mesh slips past their gills, preventing them from backing out to escape. But more often the fish sense the net, turn and swim along it. If the net is stretched tight in a straight line, they swim free right past the end, but if a curl has been set at each end they are trapped. Jae learned when and how far to turn the boat as Bill fed out the net, and as they perfected their technique, their catch increased.

Once the net was in the water, it could run afoul in countless ways and without power, the Proctors couldn't tow it out of danger. The tide pulled their net into shallow water, snagging it on submerged boulders. Logs bristling with roots and branches loomed out of the darkness to rip the fabric apart. A friend of the Proctors' was guarding his net one night when a stiff finger brushed up his back under his shirt. In sheer terror, the solo fisherman spun around and was met by a monster rearing over him in the long shadows of his dim lantern. The poor fellow received a mighty shock in the seconds it took him to figure out that the "monster" was a huge root with one tiny tendril under his shirt. Bill and Jae took turns guarding their net. The cramped, uncomfortable conditions aboard the skiff helped them stay awake.

Known as "rag-pickers," gillnetters are very familiar with every type of floating debris on the coast. Popweed, a seaweed with air-bladders which keep it afloat, and sticks collect in the mesh near the corkline and each piece must be taken out one at a time. Jae's fingers became raw with cuts that chafed on the constant layer of drying salt coating her hands, and never healed. Jellyfish adhered to the net at all depths, the worst being red jellyfish tentacles. These jellyfish defend and feed themselves with a powerful poison. Their poison doesn't hurt right away; it takes a few seconds, then a tingling starts, followed by burning and darting stings. The poison is difficult to remove. If Jae rubbed her nose, or worse her eyes, she wept. The pain is so intense it is difficult to imagine you are not going blind. Bill had to be very careful if he had to relieve himself while dealing with red jellyfish. Other fishermen told them to pour canned milk on the afflicted area, but this was more of a distraction than a cure.

Jae studied the corkline during the long hours of her watch and learned to read the dancing corks. If they shivered instead of bobbing she knew they were into a school of dogfish, a small type of shark. When dogfish hit she woke Bill and they pulled on the net together to get it into the boat as fast as possible. Dogfish writhe and twist, quickly wrapping themselves in the net. If it was a big school they spent most of the night removing them. The sharks' rough skin ripped and frayed the net. The best action was when the corks sank just below the surface, signalling a heavy catch of salmon.

The packer boat made the rounds every day to pick up Bill and Jae's catch. There was no way to keep the fish cool so it was essential to get them to the cannery as soon as possible.

After four days and nights of steady fishing, Jae was happy to see the packer coming to tow them home. She spent Friday and Saturday washing salt and fish slime out of their clothes, drying the bedding, sleeping, baking bread and reprovisioning the skiff. Sundays came too quickly and before she knew it she was crouched in the skiff once again.

Bill and Jae lived full time at Charles Creek for one year, and were hired as winter caretakers for several years thereafter. In 1929 Jae gave birth to a daughter, Patsy, and now that they were a family it really felt like home. Jae fondly recalled their life at Charles Creek in this poem:

> Away from the city's dust and heat,
> Is a little place called Charles Creek.
> A little place beside the sea
> That once was 'Home Sweet Home' to me.
>
> Charles Creek, October 16th, 1931

Bill with Patsy, Charles Creek, 1929. (PHOTO BY JAE PROCTOR)

Cannery at Charles Creek, 1929. (PHOTO BY JAE PROCTOR)

However, life in Kingcome Inlet was not always so tranquil. In 1933, during spring thaw, the little bay was transformed into a nightmarish death trap. Jae recorded the horrific night in another poem:

One day it rained so awful hard,
And the night was dark and drear
And as we all sat playing cards
I had an awful fear.

We had just crawled into our bed,
When I heard an awful roar
And when we looked outside the house,
There was snow and trees galore.

The snow came from the hill top
As the wind blew down our door
And filled up all our kitchen
From ceiling to the floor.

Bill just grabbed wee Patsy
And ran into the night
I stayed a while to don my clothes
But we sure had an awful fright.

We could hardly make it thru' the snow
For branches and trees and muck,
But at last we made our boat
By wading through the chuck.

And when we got inside it
We found it full of snow,
But we were glad to stay there,
As we had nowhere else to go....

And when the morning came at last
What an awful sight to see.
Snow and ice and dirt galore
Piled right down to the sea.

The Indian shacks and oil house,
Were gone from where they stood.
And all that was left of them
Was a few pieces of wood.

The house that we were living in
Had moved about a foot
And all the trees and honeysuckle
Were pulled up by the root.

I sure will be happy
When we can move away.
Charles Creek, March 1933

The cannery was never rebuilt. Ragnar Hanson, a logger, came to Charles Creek in 1945 and built a truck road up the valley. He logged there for about 15 years, then sold the claim to Jack Baben.

Baben logged there till 1968. Since then Charles Creek has been recovering. The debris left by the loggers has been cleared and the river planted with hatchery coho.

Charles Creek after the slide. Jae and Bill were in the house on the right. (PHOTO BY JAE PROCTOR)

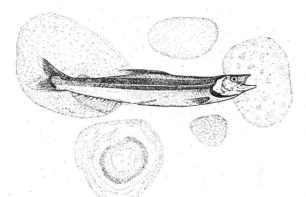

CHAPTER TWO

Now we are living on our boat
Which isn't bad for two
But there's Bill, Patsy and me
And we have a baby too.

IN 1931, BILL got a handlogging claim in Bellisle Sound, across Kingcome Inlet from Charles Creek. A handlogging claim in those days was six miles of shoreline. Bill logged spruce boomsticks. Boomsticks are long straight logs used to form a corral, or "boom" around other logs, storing them until there are enough to tow to market. The Powell River Company camp at the head of Kingcome Inlet paid Bill five dollars a log. He got an additional 25¢ a hole if he bored the boomchain holes at each end of the logs. Bill used a hand auger, which is essentially a giant corkscrew. It was gruelling work, boring a four-inch-wide hole at each end of the logs, but the Proctors were saving for a house of their own.

In 1932, Bill and Jae had put enough money aside to buy a floathouse. Floathouses are typical houses built on a raft of logs. They were used extensively by loggers, who needed to move their camps from one claim to the next. Before seaplanes, families lived where they worked and floathouses were ideal. In the summers Bill and Jae tied their floathouse in Charles Creek for the fishing season and then they moved into Bellisle for the winters to log. Jae loved her home. She kept the wood cookstove gleaming and her frugal Scottish nature made the most of what little they had.

Bill logged with Carl Stamey, who had already been in Bellisle a few years. Bellisle is a deep, comma-shaped slot in the mountains. Its steep sides trap low-lying clouds and they pile in there like damp blankets. Bellisle's sombre, dark mood made Jae sad and lonely, so they towed their floathouse into low-lying Moore Bay and then around the corner into Shawl Bay. It is easy to change scenery and look for neighbours in a floathouse. However, no anchorage is perfect. West winds rocked the floathouse so hard Jae had to tie guylines on the hanging gas lanterns to prevent them from spilling and hitting the walls.

By fishing, logging, camp watching and mending nets, Jae and Bill soon had enough money to buy a 32-foot gillnetter. The wooden boat was stoutly named *Helga Herman*, but Bill, who enjoyed gambling, decided to rename her *Zev* after a racehorse that had once brought him good fortune. The Proctors' new boat had a solid cabin, one they could actually stand in, and it was powered by a one cylinder Frisbee gas engine. Jae loved the cosy *Zev*. Indeed, the boat must have felt like a luxury liner compared to the open skiff. Instead of huddling and shivering beneath a damp tarp, Jae now watched the net from her perch beside a woodstove. *Zev* was a home on the sea.

After two years of gillnetting with *Zev*, Bill and Jae took the Department of Fisheries patrol position for the Bond Sound-Thompson Sound area in Tribune Channel. The Ahta River in Bond Sound and the Kakweikan in Thompson produced important commercial runs of salmon, particularly pink salmon. As the

Fisheries patrolman, Bill was hired to count how many salmon returned to the rivers each year to spawn. These numbers are important, and each year is different. With pink salmon, for example, the big runs are every other year. In the Mainland those are on the even years. In addition to these cycles, no one ever knows how many salmon will survive out in the ocean. Sometimes there is low survivorship, and very few adults return to spawn; the Department of Fisheries uses the number of fish going upriver to estimate how many fish can be harvested the year their offspring return. It is an imprecise science at best, and the only hard numbers are the counts made by patrollers.

It was also Bill's responsibility to keep boats from poaching in the protected waters at the river mouths. In an effort to conserve salmon stocks, Fisheries was beginning to prohibit fishing at the mouths of some heavily spawned rivers. Thousands of salmon often school in the deltas, waiting for rain to raise water levels in the rivers. When the water is too low the fish can't make it over steep falls, and the access between pools dries up. In dry years it is

Zev in Leroy Bay, CA. 1930. (Photo by Jae Proctor)

easy to wipe out entire generations of fish by fishing too hard at the mouths of the rivers, and so fishing closures began.

Salmon don't enter their rivers all at once; they come in waves for several months and so Jae and Bill visited the Ahta and Kakweikan rivers every few days throughout the migrations. Jae became familiar with Tribune Channel's dark, remote beauty. The steep-sided mountains plunge straight down, echoing whale blows, wolf howls and the voices of loons crying out for companionship. The couple walked miles of stream bed, counting fish. These valleys are wild places, home to grizzly bears, deer and wolves.

Jae had considerable doubts about walking through the feeding grounds of bears and wolves with her daughter on her hip, but Bill assured her the predators would be too busy feeding on salmon to be much of a threat. They made plenty of noise to warn of their approach and never had any problems.

In 1933, Jae had given birth to a son, but the baby only lived a few days. By early spring of 1934 she knew she was pregnant again and they took the Fisheries patrol for the Port Neville-Adams River area off Johnstone Strait. They had sold the floathouse and were living on *Zev*. In Port Neville, at the home of a midwife, Jae gave birth to another child and they named him Billy.

With two children Jae wanted to move onto land, to grow gardens and let her children run, so the Proctors bought the White Beach Trading Post Company that autumn and moved to Freshwater Bay, Swanson Island, on the southeastern edge of Blackfish Sound. The purchase included 176 acres of forest, a store, a home, the post office, several other buildings, floats and a fishbuying business. It was a big move for the little family.

Far more numerous than today, the big canneries on the coast were centrally located. While they attempted to be as close as possible to the prime fishing grounds, their placement was decided by the availability of plentiful fresh water, and often they were several hours away from the best fishing. There was no ice in those days, so the fish had to be collected off the boats every night. Rather than waste a half-day's fishing running to and from the cannery, the fishermen preferred to sell their catches to buyers, who ran their businesses on the fishing grounds. It was better for

The house, post office and general store in Freshwater Bay, 1930s. (PHOTO BY JAE PROCTOR)

the canneries to send boats out to the fishbuyers every evening, instead of chasing the fishermen around. The Proctors became fishbuyers and sold to ABC Packers in Knight Inlet, one of the biggest cannery operations on the coast.

Bill Proctor was pleased to finally have a real home for his wife and children. There was land for gardens, poultry and a cow, and they could make a good living right there without being constantly on the move. Bill Proctor was a well-liked, good-natured man. He worked hard all his life and his life reflected just that. His first job, when he was 15, was packing "a preacher's belongings" over a mule trail into Coal Harbour on the west coast of Vancouver Island for ten dollars. Now, while it was nothing elaborate, he had worked steadily, saved, and built a good life for himself and his family. The British Columbia coast was a land of opportunity for anybody willing to work.

Bill fished all day and then bought fish in the evening, while Jae ran the store and post office. They were doing very well, but there were those who felt the fishbuyer shouldn't be out fishing as well. These grumblers had been selling to the trading post before the Proctors bought it. Bill couldn't afford to lose their fish to the buyer in nearby Double Bay, so as a compromise he sold his gillnet and rigged *Zev* for trolling. Essentially, he was starting all over again, in learning a different method of catching salmon.

No fishing method is easy and Bill quickly noticed that just dropping hooks over the side and dragging them around didn't catch fish. What he already knew from gillnetting was that success depended on the details. With each fish that came aboard, Bill took note of the tide, the colour of the water, the condition of the lure, his position, his speed and countless other factors. His memory was sharp and he loved the challenge. Gradually, he got the hang of it. At first he simply followed the others, but he soon developed a fishing plan of his own. *Zev* became one of the top spring salmon boats in Blackfish Sound. Predictably, his success became a problem.

Fishermen as a group have always been keen on voicing complaints and the possibilities are endless. The water colour is wrong, the tides are haywire, the fish have moved or stray electricity on the boat is scaring them off. While all these things bother fishermen, the greatest injustice is being outfished by a newcomer. When the other boats unloaded in the evening, their day was over, but Bill's was only half done. He helped unload the other boats, weighed and sorted the catches; then he did the books and loaded the cannery boats. Despite this extra work, the fishermen decided it was simply "unfair" that Proctor both caught and bought fish. Had he been a lousy fisherman it is doubtful they would have raised the issue, but he was good and a newcomer to boot.

The men gave Bill so much grief about the fishbuyer catching all the fish that he relented. His business depended on their loyalty, because there was plenty of buying competition in the vicinity of Blackfish Sound. Mike Davis bought fish in Double Bay, there was a camp in Baronet Pass, Al Hood was set up on the north end of Swanson Island in Yokohama Bay and Spence Turner had a fish-buying station in Mitchell Bay on Malcolm Island. Bill simply couldn't afford to drive fishermen away. So he stripped *Zev*, sold the trolling gear for ten dollars and stayed on the dock.

Proctor's Fish Camp, as it was renamed, treated the fishermen well. To entice boats, Bill offered free moorage, and he picked up fresh supplies and groceries for the fishermen on his mail runs. Most importantly, Bill made sure his prices were competitive:

Humps (pink salmon) — 5¢ each
Dogs (chum salmon) — 25¢ each
Coho — 5¢ a pound
Red Springs (chinook) — 7¢ a pound
White Springs — 2¢ a pound

Gas was selling for 19¢ a gallon so making a profit wasn't guaranteed for the fishermen. Fishing has always been a hard living for the people who own and operate their own boats.

ABC Packers, which bought Proctor's fish, was located in Glendale Cove in Knight Inlet. ABC canned most of their salmon, salting only the chums and white springs. Appearance is everything and white springs, although equally delicious, were less valued than their pink-fleshed counterparts. In fact, they were worth less than any other salmon.

Spring salmon flesh has a wide range of colours, from deep red to pale pink; white spring meat looks like halibut and still others are marbled pink and white. Some say this is due to variations in diet, but the prevailing opinion is that each population has its own distinctive colour. Different runs within the same river can be completely different colours. Both opinions may be correct, as the white springs may be a population that simply does not feed on the pink, shrimp-like euphausiids. Salmon farmers later discovered that feeding salmon pellets produces grey flesh and so they put pink dye in the feed to turn the meat pink.

While he missed fishing, Bill adjusted to life on the dock. In the summer months Freshwater Bay was a thriving little community. Everyone knew everyone and they all kept an eye out for each other. There were times when staying in the bay was almost as exciting as being out fishing.

One day, a strong northwest gale kept most of the boats at the dock. At about 6:00 AM, one of the boats caught fire and smoke started pouring out of it. The boat's skipper had woken earlier, seen the day was no good for fishing, turned up his stove against the westerly and fallen back asleep. For reasons he couldn't later explain he'd also thrown his pillow on top of the stove. When he opened his eyes for the second time, all he could see was smoke and he scrambled for the door. Just as he opened it someone coming to his rescue sprayed him with a fire extinguisher. Panicked, the fisherman turned to get out through the skylight, but was hit in the face with a washtub of water. Finally, he crawled out the door on his hands and knees, covered in extinguishing foam, pillow feathers and water.

On another occasion, Stan Prout on *Alice Mac* hit Pearse Reef off Alert Bay and his boat sank. On his way home with the mail, Bill found old Stan sitting in the crosstree of his mast, holding onto his AM radio. Bill manoeuvred close enough for Stan to jump aboard and just as he did, the boat rolled over into deeper water. Stan wouldn't have survived in the boiling pass and was thankful Bill had spotted him.

Buster Lansdowne was another fisherman who sold to Proctor. Well known for his fearlessness on the water, Lansdowne took his boat *Kathleen* away out to sea in any kind of weather. He fished until it was too rough and then just drifted in the big seas. He kept the water out with a plug in the stove pipe and caulking around the door. To make coffee, when drifting in huge seas, Buster and his crew wedged themselves into the bow, cradling the primus stove and kettle on top. His deckhands always had lots of stories to tell. One reported that Buster waited until they were bucking their way over the wild and infamous Nahwitti Bar to climb into the crosstree and paint the mast.

Lansdowne used to ferry travelling salesmen around to the logging camps. He had a unique, two-masted boat called *Lapaloma*. One nervous salesman demanded to know if Buster was sure he knew where all the rocks were, before he would get on the boat. Lansdowne assured him, that yes, he knew every rock, and off they went. They didn't get far before *Lapaloma* smashed into a rock.

As Buster told it, the nervous salesman whined, "I thought you said you knew where all the rocks were."

Buster grinned and said, "Yup, and that's just the first one."

These men prided themselves on being tough. Competing took their minds off the dangers and the pain. Herbert Ray's motor quit as his boat *O.Bill* was pulling away from the float at Freshwater Bay. The season was over and he was heading south for the winter. When the motor quit the boat was headed straight for a rock bluff on Flower Island. Without the motor there was no way to stop her, so Ray ran up on the bow and put his leg out to protect his boat, smashing one of his feet between the bowstem and the rock. The foot was a mess, but the boat was safe. Then he got his motor going and went on his way. It took him four days to get home to Vancouver, and when he finally saw a doctor, he had seven broken bones.

The years from 1934 to 1938 were happy ones for the Proctor family. Freshwater Bay hummed to the tune of a well-run business and a growing family. Patsy was her mother's little shadow. She pitched in happily with the chores: cooking mush for her little brother, dusting and carefully tending her miniature flower box. During the busy fishing season, she could be depended on to watch over the baby.

The little redhead was adventurous and full of his own ideas. Like all three-year-old boys, Billy tried to imitate the men around him. On one occasion it nearly killed him. Vastly impressed with

Patsy and Billy. (PHOTO BY JAE PROCTOR)

25

Billy and friends, Freshwater Bay, CA. 1937. (PHOTO BY JAE PROCTOR)

the way fishermen drank from water jugs balanced on their shoulders, Billy was determined to do the same. He found a jug, looped a chubby little finger through the handle and managed to get it to his mouth. A big swig of kerosene slid down his throat. He turned blue, then purple, until he was forced to vomit the deadly fuel. It took him several days to recover from that.

Billy was fascinated by all things to do with the sea, and sometimes he played with the incoming tide. He'd sit down at the water's edge at low tide and remain motionless as the tide came in and crept up his body. He wouldn't move until the cold salt water invaded his nostrils. His tuft of red hair afloat yards from shore was a strange sight, and more than one man dashed to the rescue, yelling, "Hey Proctor, your kid's in the water!"

Familiar with his son's fixation with the tide, Bill would glance at the situation and yell back, "It's OK. His eyeballs are still showing."

Some of the men who fished for Proctor's camp lived year round in the Mainland. "Two Gun" Brown was an old cowboy who lived on his boat in Simoom Sound and Echo Bay, where he watched camp during the winter. In summer when he trolled, he tied up at

Freshwater Bay. Billy, accustomed to Scottish cleanliness, was very intrigued by the state of Two Gun, a self-proclaimed "dirty old fart." However, that man had stories. Sitting in a small space that had never been cleaned, Billy listened, fascinated, to the life of a cowboy.

Two Gun Brown longlined for dogfish and every night, as the man cut out the valuable livers that he sold for their high oil content, the boy would come to listen to stories. One night, Brown came in looking shaken. "Well," he started, "as I was pulling the gear aboard, a giant octopus leg came waving in over the side and it was followed by another and they just kept comin'."

The cowboy grabbed his bait-cutting knife and started slicing off the legs as they came into the boat and caught hold of him. He thought he was going to lose the battle as there seemed no end to the creature. Billy eyed the deep knife cuts in the rail all the way around the cockpit and the chunks of octopus legs six inches across that lay everywhere. Sleep was a long time coming that night as he thought about the terror of being dragged overboard by such a monster.

Fred Mason built a homestead in a bay west of the Proctors' place and grew mushrooms. He was gone before Billy could form any memories of him, but when he was five, a polite, elderly man with a patch over one eye, named Bud Wilson, asked to move into

Two Gun Brown's boat, with a cable around the cabin to hold it together. (PHOTO BY JAE PROCTOR)

Mason's house. Bill thought that would be fine, but as soon as Wilson got settled, the old gentleman started up a still and began selling moonshine. Bill was angry that the old man hadn't told him what he was up to and he told Wilson to get out. He was not going to have a bunch of drunks coming and going around his family.

Wilson moved to Beaver Cove, but he returned one day looking for a fight. Bellowing, Wilson looked mean coming up the dock with the black patch over his lost eye and young Billy was sure he must be a pirate. He was impressed no end when his dad picked Wilson up, threw him back on his boat and cut it loose. There was no point in waiting for the police, as they didn't have a boat.

Fishermen were the major source of entertainment for the children. In particular, they were fond of Whilkey, who lived right in Freshwater Bay in a little shack. Billy often helped Whilkey with his firewood and in return the man told Billy and Patsy stories. Not having an outhouse, Whilkey used the one down on the float. The trouble was that the other fishermen always wanted to talk when they saw Whilkey coming down the dock. Whilkey didn't want to be rude and the children loved it when he tore down the ramp, bellowing "Don't stop me!" on his charge by to the outhouse.

Every spring Whilkey put his boat on the grid and painted her green and white. He only had one brush and he got a little

Whilkey with Patsy and Billy. (PHOTO BY JAE PROCTOR)

distracted occasionally, dipping into the wrong can. Whilkey's boat always looked a little odd, with green streaks in the white and white streaks in the green, but he didn't seem to mind. He told the children he was "just dolling her up." One morning the Royal Canadian Mounted Police came and took Whilkey away to the "old men's home," and Billy and Patsy cried at the loss of their friend.

Busy as Bill was with his business he made time for his son, and he left the boy with fond memories of the times they spent together fishing from their rowboat. They went out jigging greenling and then, because Jae would not permit fish in her kitchen, they fried up their catch together in the post office on the primus stove.

In 1941 Japanese-Canadians were imprisoned in internment camps. If they were fishermen, their boats were taken away. This was a major blow not only to the fishermen, but to Bill and Jae, who bought their catches. The 29 Japanese-Canadian fishermen of Blackfish Sound were among the best in the fleet, and Bill had relied heavily on their catches. To keep up his business, he had to diversify. He began buying clams.

Bill hired a man to run *Zev* around the Mainland to collect sacks of clams from the diggers. When this man failed to return from a trip up to Echo Bay, Bill contacted the police in Alert Bay. Because the police didn't have their own boat, they came out in the Game Department's vessel *P.G.D. II*. The search party checked the obvious places for the missing man, then stopped at the Proctors. When Jae invited them in for tea, they jokingly asked her if she "knew" where the man was.

Jae had a reputation for clairvoyant dreams. Most people were sceptical of her ability to "see," but the men figured it wouldn't hurt to ask. As it turned out she had dreamed about the lost man only the night before. Jae said she didn't really know where he was, but in her dream, he had been walking the rocky beach of a tiny island with his feet strangely huge. The policemen nodded politely and took off to resume their search. They found the poor man on a tiny islet named House Island. He had wrapped his feet in several clam gunny sacks to keep his toes from freezing. The police made a point of talking with Jae more often after that.

Bill Proctor with Billy and his pet chicken, 1939. (PHOTO BY JAE PROCTOR)

Jae wrote a long poem to celebrate the good times they shared:

Pat and Billy sure are good
The fairies think they are
As each nite they leave a sticker
Or else a chocolate bar.

They want to know how Santa gets here.
Has he an aeroplane or sled
A steamer or a sailboat, and why
Does he come when they are in bed?

We have a real nice fir tree
All trimmed up nice and bright
With tinsel, bulbs and candles
That we'll light up tonight....

Billy got a train that runs
And a kitten that stands up

But what we played with most was
A thing called Pluto the pup....

The turkey's in the oven
There are pies and cake galore.
And we don't know just how many
Will be here, maybe a dozen or more....

Well Xmas day is over
For another year
And I wonder if next Xmas
That we will all be here....

Christmas Day, 1937

The last verse seemed strange, but two months later Jae's beloved Patsy died of spinal meningitis. Her parents suspected that the deadly disease found its way to remote Freshwater Bay on the mail. Patsy had loved playing "post office" with the empty envelopes. Deep within Jae sprang a freshet of sorrow that never completely healed. In her poems she described her loved ones as flowers. When her daughter died she wrote:

[God picked]...a little half open rose bud.

Freshwater Bay, February 1938

Earlier, when her second child, an infant son, had died shortly after his birth, she neatly penned:

[God]...picked the newest rose.

Alert Bay, September 1933

And then in February 1942, tear stains blurred the blue ink of Jae's journal as she wrote:

God came again to our garden
And took our Daddy away

And we are awful lonely
But we'll meet again some day.

It sure is an empty garden
With all three gone away....

The freshet swelled to a hidden torrent. Jae had two daughters from a previous marriage, but they were far away and her only contact with them was through letters. So now there was only one sprout remaining in her garden of life, a rugged little vine:

wee red haired Billy
Freshwater Bay, February 5th, 1942

Billy in the garden at Freshwater Bay, CA. 1938. (PHOTO BY JAE PROCTOR)

Chapter Three

He sure can handle a rowboat
Tho' he is only five,
And he loves it on the float
When the fishermen arrive.

A WOMAN'S ROLE in the wilderness depends a great deal on whom she is with. If she is by herself she can take risks. If she is with a man, she generally doesn't have to. But if she is alone with a small child, she can't afford to. Jae was determined not to leave Billy an orphan. With her husband at her side, she had tended their home, their children and the store. Now it was all up to her. Fortunately, fishbuying was something Jae could take on. If Bill had been a logger, or many other things, she would have had to make some tough decisions. As it was, Jae had the option of trying to fill Bill's shoes. It took several years, but in time she found them a good fit.

Pearly Sherdahl, who owned the lively Minstrel Island Hotel, was a kind soul and he made every effort to help Jae out. Minstrel Island is a few miles east of Freshwater Bay, in the mouth of Knight Inlet. Sherdahl brought Jae logs for firewood and every second Sunday he payed a social call. Over a cup of tea he gave Jae the latest gossip and news, and made sure she and the boy were doing OK. It was Pearly who salvaged *Zev*, patched her up and left her safely on the beach for Jae to sell. *Zev* changed hands for $65.

By all accounts "wee Billy" was a headstrong boy, determined to do things his own way. Keeping him in one piece required constant effort and this vigilance distracted Jae from dwelling on her circumstances. Her son forced her to maintain the routine of their life, pushing grieving aside. At times, another young woman, Bernice Whitmore, known as Benny, stayed at Freshwater Bay to help out. Benny's parents sold fish to Jae off their troller. Before Benny's arrival Jae was troubled by the silence: the house was no longer filled with her daughter's chatter and Bill's deep voice. Benny brought life and laughter back to the island. And she loved little Billy dearly.

Benny Whitmore and Billy, aboard the packer IZUMI 5, *going to Alert Bay.* (PHOTO BY JAE PROCTOR)

34

Before turning the boy loose to roam the docks, Jae and Benny buckled him into his life jacket, but he hated the bulky contraption and wriggled out of it as soon as he was free of them. Jae knew that with one small slip she could be completely alone. One afternoon Bruno Sevnin was on his way up to the store when he happened to look down as he stepped from one float to the next. There, lying on the bottom, was a little boy. Racing up the dock moments before, Billy had fallen into the water. Bruno dropped to his knees and could just reach the child whom he pulled unconscious from the water. Young Billy was barely alive. Another handful of seconds and he would have drowned.

As Jae didn't have the resources to maintain both Freshwater Bay and a place in town, Billy was not sent to school. Instead, Jae ordered correspondence schooling. When the material arrived she sat the boy down and laid the formidable stack of papers before him on the table. One look was enough. Billy bolted for the door and hid in the woods for the rest of the day. The situation was hopeless. Billy refused to do schoolwork. He gleefully recalls, "Mum just packed up the books and returned them by mail."

Jae, however, found a way to teach the boy to read. She bought him a two-volume dictionary and Billy learned on his own. Heber Green on the mission boat *Columbia* helped considerably, by loaning Billy books he knew would prove irresistible. A favourite was Roderick Haig-Brown's classic, *Saltwater Summer*, about the adventure of two boys becoming commercial fishermen on the B.C. coast.

Anything about fishing caught Billy's attention. Like most coastal children, Billy was jigging cod before he could read. By age five, he was selling his catch to the Chinese men at the ABC Cannery in Glendale. Every evening, when the packer came down from the cannery to pick up the salmon from Proctor's Fish Camp, Billy placed his galvanized tub full of cod aboard as well. The next night, when the boat returned, Billy received his pay and got his tub back. The succulent, fresh, white flesh of cod was welcomed by the cannery workers, who endured miserable living conditions and very poor rations.

When he was ready to catch bigger fish, Billy took two pink salmon out of a fish bin, cut them up and baited several hooks,

First boat, 1940. (PHOTO BY JAE PROCTOR)

spaced along a heavy line. He laid the set line out on the bottom of the bay along the dock. "All hell broke loose" when a 70-pound halibut sucked in one of the chunks of bait. With great difficulty, making sure his legs didn't get tangled in the line, the young fisherman dragged his catch along the float to the beach. A 70-pound halibut can easily pull a small boy under water, but Billy landed the fish, which was nearly twice his size. Proudly, he sliced the halibut into thick, delicious steaks and sold them for ten cents apiece; the thrill of success was not lost on him.

Billy would have liked to fish all day, but he had chores to do, so he rigged a rod holder for his bamboo pole. His baited line continued to fish on its own, while Billy sawed firewood or tended the garden. Attached to the tip of the pole was a bell that rang out whenever a fish bit. One evening, the bell erupted into a frenzied rhythm. Billy heard it from inside the house and shot out the door, leaving it to slam unheeded. When he grabbed the homemade pole his heart pounded at the sight of something big and silvery flashing wildly at the end of his line. This was no cod or even a halibut; it was a man's catch — a salmon.

Landing the 12-pound coho was sheer heaven to Billy, but he couldn't figure out how he'd hooked it. He knew no salmon would bite a chunk of bait lying on the bottom. Shiny moving lures were needed to catch a coho. For years Billy wondered how he had managed to hook that fish. Old Ed Hansen off *Galley Bay* (*Vianndot* in those days) knew. Ed had caught the fish at the end of the day and carefully kept it alive in a bucket, until he returned to Freshwater Bay for the night. There, as the other fishermen watched, he carefully pulled up Billy's line, making sure not to jiggle the bell, attached the fish and slipped it back into the water. Then he sat back with his friends and watched the show.

The coho wasn't the only one to get hooked that evening. Billy was no longer content to fish off the docks now that he'd had a taste of some real action. Despite what his mother had to say on the subject, Billy set out in his rowboat to become a commercial fisherman at seven years of age.

Freshwater Bay lies at the north end of Blackney Pass, a major marine artery connecting Johnstone Strait to Queen Charlotte Strait. Whirlpools, slick upwellings and rough tidelines are formed as the straits flood and ebb against the constricting shorelines of the pass. It is not a calm place to go rowing. Swift currents could easily overpower two small oars and sweep a little boy away.

The first day he headed out, Billy chose a spoon off the rack at his mum's store and took off. Rowing steadily close to shore, he dragged the lure around on a hand line. The line was tied to a wooden pole sticking straight up with a tiny brass bell on the end. Billy loved that bell; it made his boat seem more like the big trollers with their bells on the ends of the trolling poles. It wasn't long before a mature spring salmon spied the spoon and struck. Had the boy's boat been bigger, the line would have snapped because Billy couldn't row and play the fish at the same time. However, the little rowboat acted as the drag and the salmon was unable to break free. Billy was just barely able to guide his catch to the beach and land it there.

He cleaned it right away and was a little disappointed to find it was a white spring, but it weighed 42 pounds, a fine fish by any standard. He sold the salmon to his mother and bought more gear with the money.

Being able to row around in his own boat allowed Billy to become acquainted with Joe, the humpback whale that lived around Freshwater Bay. Billy saw Joe almost every day and got to know his habits well. The whale would appear at slack tide to feed on the big schools of herring that swirled in huge, dark clouds in those days. When the whale surfaced through a school of herring, the little fish rained off his head. Occasionally Joe entered Freshwater Bay and swam beneath the floats or raised his flukes in the kelp, pulling the long fronds into the sun. When the tide started to run hard again, Joe would stay in the back eddy by the kelp and go to sleep. Billy watched him lying there with just his blowhole above water, puffing now and then, his belly full of herring.

As time passed, Billy felt confident enough around Joe to row right up to the 50-foot whale. The little boat didn't seem to disturb him and leaning over the side, Billy could see Joe's eye peering back, his long mouth fixed in an apparent smile. Billy let the rowboat drift against the giant resting mammal and laid his small hand on the immense back. The whale never flinched, perceiving no threat from the gentle creature touching him. Joe probably classified Billy and his boat as just another duck.

The first boat from which Billy fished commercially, 1941. (PHOTO BY JAE PROCTOR)

Joe sometimes had the company of another humpback whale. They would breach, roll and slap the water with their flukes, and to the boy, it looked like fun. Once, when killer whales were after him, Joe came into the bay and lay close by the floats. This discouraged the orcas and they took off to attack another humpback. They ate only what they needed and left. Unfortunately, that whale could not recover from the attack and Billy watched the poor creature bleed to death over a period of four days.

★★★

As Jae could not muster the courage to venture out in a boat alone, she was dependent on her neighbours for mail and supplies. Her closest neighbours were Bob Davis, a fisherman on *Rusty* and Rod Williams, a logger who periodically ran his 32-foot cruiser to Alert Bay. If Jae hung a white cloth from her clothesline, they would stop their boats out in front of the bay long enough for Billy to row out to them with a shopping list and ten dollars. The money covered the groceries and in the evening they idled out front again until Billy came to pick up the goods.

Freshwater Bay

Well, here it's fishing season again
The busiest time of the year
Some boats are here already
Waiting for the fish to appear.

Some fishermen are lucky
Some have no luck at all
I only hope that big run comes
So we won't be broke this fall.

Billy caught some rock cod
Just the other day
He put them in the fish scale
Then demanded his pay.

Some boats are awfully clean
Not a bit of dirt to see
With everything so tidy
They sure look nice to me.

Other boats they are so dirty
With dirt and muck and junk
Things are thrown most everywhere
And their grub lies on the bunk.

When the fish are running good
And each man gets his share
They never seem to worry much
Or seem to have a care.

But when the fish aren't biting
And they've come in with a skunk
They seem to get cross and cranky
I know it is the bunk.

This fishing is a gamble
For the men as well as us.
And if we do lose sometimes
Why make such a fuss?

Now my story is ended
About the fishermen here
Maybe I'll tell you more
About them all next year.

For 20 years, from 1942 to 1962, Jae ran the camp on her own. The fishbuying business usually brought in $600 to $700 profit a year and with that Jae and Billy were able to survive. One season they only made $147. The biggest annual expense was their purchase of oil for the stove. They burned a barrel a month during the winter and the barrels cost $7.50 to $8 apiece.

At first, only a few men sold to Jae and they did it because they felt sorry for her. But she paid fair price, cash every night, and so new boats gradually began to queue at the widow Proctor's dock. When the season started up, Jae offered a loan in the form of food and fuel to get them started. Only one boat, skippered by Elmer Krooks, never returned to pay for the $30 worth of goods she had given him. Most fishermen were too independent to accept Jae's loan, but they liked her for offering. Jae was kind-hearted but tough. If someone dared suggest her scales were off, she told them there was another buyer in the next bay and the men liked her for that, too. Christmas time always brought evidence of their esteem, with over 150 cards wishing her well.

The first few years were difficult, and like any family which has suffered loss, Jae and Billy found that Christmas was one of the hardest times.

I remember Christmas of 1938. We were all together that year. But by 1939, my sister was gone. Christmas of 1940 and 1941 were good times. There was Mum and Dad and me and folks would come from miles around to our house. There were

Jae slinging fish, Freshwater Bay, 1940. (COLLECTION OF JAE PROCTOR)

around 34 of us that sat down for dinner on those Christmas days. We always ate at 3:00 PM so folks could go home before dark. But most stayed overnight on their boats. Some came all the way from Glendale Cove in Knight Inlet, 45 miles away. I remember 1940 as one of my best Christmases. I got a sailboat. It was about three feet long and white, made of steel, and it sailed real good.

I remember in 1941, we had a real bad storm just before Christmas and Santa never made it. All I found under the tree in the morning was a note from Santa saying it was too rough. Little did we know that it would be the last Christmas we would be all together.

I sure can remember 1942, just Mum and me and old Duffy, a neighbour. There was three feet of snow, no firewood, and we had to pack water 500 feet. But we made it through and many more after that. In 1943 just Mum, me and Duffy and two more folks came around. I remember 1944 real well as that was the first year I trapped and I had made money handtrolling. I saved all I could and I got a ride into Alert Bay just before Christmas and got Mum a nice box of candy. It was a nice wooden box. I still have it. Mum always kept cards and odds and ends in it. That was the first time I went shopping on my own — what a big event for me.

If it was a nice day, Mum and I would row out to Flower Island and walk around. Mum loved Flower Island. It was Mum that named the island for the wild roses, paintbrush, columbine and other flowers that grew all around it. But if it was a stormy day, we would stay home and Mum would make some fudge or something good to eat. If there was snow on the ground we would make ice cream.

Jae and Billy's meals were modest. Often they had pancakes for supper or bread soaked in milk, and Jello was a mainstay. Billy shot his first deer when he was eight from inside the kitchen window and from then on he kept them in venison. Jae canned the good bits for them and gave the bones to the dogs. She felt strongly about not adopting what she saw as the habits of the poor, and lived by a strict, self-imposed code. She would never eat broken cookies, wild game or even fish. If her son wanted to eat fish he could cook it out in the post office as he had done with his dad. In addition, Billy was not allowed to wear torn clothing. This must have been a challenge as he constantly roamed the forest and beach.

With each year, Billy grew more capable and took on more chores, and as a fishbuyer, Jae was gaining a solid reputation. During one particularly good fishing opening, boats from other areas converged on Blackfish Sound. Since none of them had ice aboard to keep their fish, they all had to find a local buyer, and when the number of boats selling to her doubled from 25 to 50, Jae ran out of cash. It was frustrating to her not to be able to take advantage of the additional fish. Then one of her steady fishermen offered her a loan of $500. That was a lot of money in those days, and she hated to take it, but she was about to accept when an even more generous offer was made. A group of highliners dubbed "the Nanaimo Gang," told her not to bother paying them every night. She could just settle with them at the end of the season. At one point they trusted her with $3,000 of their hard-earned income.

Jae and Billy, Freshwater Bay. (COLLECTION OF JAE PROCTOR)

Fishboats at Freshwater Bay, during the time Jae was buying fish. (COLLECTION OF JAE PROCTOR)

The Nanaimo Gang earned their highliner status by trying new ways of fishing. When there were no fish near shore, they moved out and set their lines deeper. If fishing was poor, they didn't quit by noon which was the common practice; they continued looking for fish or awaited the "bite." Fishing was as competitive then as now, but without sounders, secret radio channels, plotters or seaplanes there was a lot more guesswork. In the end, nothing beat persistence.

This is how the first flasher came to be what it is today. In 1944 a fisherman, Delmont Buck in Double Bay, got the idea to make a flasher to attract fish better than a spoon by itself. It worked and at first all flashers were homemade, of brass. A sheet of brass spoon metal was eight by twelve inches and you could get it in different thicknesses. Eighteen gauge was the thickest, 20 and 22 gauge were thinner.

The first flashers were made by cutting a sheet in half lengthwise. Some guys cut them square, others cut one end 3½ inches wide and the other 4½ inches. As far as I know, Blackfish Sound was the first place flashers were used and these were the original Blackfish Sound flashers. Soon there were many different patterns. Because they were made of brass, we had to polish them every day.

At first we joined two together and they just weaved back and forth. We couldn't make them spin back in those days because there were no ball-bearing swivels.

The first chrome I saw was in 1955 and the first spinning flasher was called a Kelp Kutter. Then in 1958 the Abe and Al was the hot item. Then along came the Gulf Flasher, the Yuculta, the Nootka, Nanaimo, Ucluelet. At first these did not spin, but soon they got them to spin too. Now it's the Hot Spot, Big Shooter, Oki, and the Pal Sockeye.

From 1943 to 1947 Billy fished commercially from a small rowboat built in Scott Cove by Carl Wal, using a technique taught him by an old friend of his dad's. Sam Charlie from the Native village at New Vancouver came out to White Beach Pass every

Flashers. Three big ones, l. to r.: Squaw Foot, Blackfish Sound, Kelp Kutter. Small rounded one in centre: Erickson Wobbler. Diamond-shaped one above Erickson: Backman Wobbler. (PHOTO BY ALEXANDRA MORTON)

summer to harvest and dry his fish for the winter and, when Billy was old enough, he taught the boy how to fish Kwakiutl style, using the tide. The method was ideal for the young fisherman.

Billy would row out to a kelp bed close to the swift waters of the pass. There he tied his bow line around several slippery, round bull-kelp heads. A larger boat would have torn the kelp's holdfasts free from the rocky bottom, but Billy's little rowboat held securely. He attached his spoon with a length of Donegal cutty hunk (a green, three-strand linen twine) to a small wooden gillnet float and set the float adrift on the tide far beyond the kelp forest. When he ran out of line, he pulled slow and steady, hand over hand as Sam Charlie had taught him. The combined effect of the tide and the pulling caused the spoon to wobble enticingly.

When Billy hooked a salmon, the line often got tangled in the kelp, but a few fish made it into the boat. Billy became a regular inhabitant of the kelp bed and sat for hours in thick summer fog. His best day was six fish. Killer whales ghosted by, hunting the same fish as the boy. It was exciting when the five-foot fin of a male killer whale surfaced at the edge of the kelp and the whale's breath dampened his face.

Billy saved enough money to purchase a 12-foot skiff built in Double Bay and a 2½ hp Johnson outboard. With this boat, he could "look" for fish instead of waiting for them to come to him and he was able to fish a proper handline set-up. As the boat putted slowly along, two "mainlines" ran into the water, one on either side, with five-pound weights spaced evenly to the ends. Attached at each weight was a length of cutty hunk towing a spoon. This allowed Billy to fish eight hooks at a time. He worked this boat for four years with increasing success.

Aye Aye was Billy's first commercially rigged troller. He bought the 27-foot boat for $2,200 in October 1951. He was 17 and knew he had made it into the big time. *Aye Aye* was not built for comfort, looks or speed. The seven hp engine was reliable, but the dull grey boat was "rotten as hell." Billy worked hard to fix her up, replacing punky boards and painting her a crisp white. She had a tiny bunk and no stove; Billy just barely fit in the cabin. It could have been made more comfortable, but some boats seem designed to keep their skippers awake at the wheel through sheer discomfort. This boat brought him the freedom to really move around and it sheltered him from the weather.

Three seasons later Billy bought an ancient 36-foot troller, *Sea Gull*, for $1,200. He wasn't interested in the hull; he bought her for the 1018 Easthope engine which he put in *Aye Aye*. Billy stripped *Sea Gull* and sold her for $500 to a friend who really wanted her.

Now that Billy was mobile he had to learn to deal with the unexpected. The first lesson came when he was 22 as he rode the big swells of an April westerly on his way to Alert Bay. It was blowing about 35 mph, which is enough to kick up a big sea. He thought he'd made it through the worst of it when he went over a big wave and came down on a deadhead. Deadheads are a mariner's worst nightmare. Hidden among the waves, these half-sunk, vertically floating logs can barely be seen from the surface.

The impact cracked a plank and the boat started to take on water. There was a hand pump on deck, so Billy began dashing back and forth between the pump and the steering wheel. He'd pump furi-

Fishing, AYE AYE, *1953.* (COLLECTION OF JAE PROCTOR)

ously until the boat veered too far off course, then race to the wheel, give it a few turns and run back to the pump. Since he was not able to pump continuously, the water came in faster than he could get rid of it.

On one of his visits to the wheel he made a hurried call to Alert Bay Coast Guard on the AM phone to tell them he was sinking and that he would keep the boat close to shore in case she went down. He couldn't swim, but figured he might be able to make it a short distance if he had to. As the water rose, the flywheel started to throw it all over the cabin. Billy took off his shirt and wrapped it around the magneto to try to keep it dry and functioning. The Easthope engine never missed a beat and when it looked as though he was going to make it to Alert Bay, he radioed the Coast Guard and asked them to arrange for the ways at the shipyard to be let down. When he got there, he ran the boat right up onto the cradle with a foot of water over the floor. He'd just about lost his boat.

Later, when Billy hit a rock at Bold Head, *Aye Aye* had to sit on it till high tide. Bill Scow came by and asked if he was planning on copper painting the bottom while he was up there. Billy was embarrassed.

Although each fisherman must discover for himself or herself how to catch fish, a great deal can be learned dockside by just listening. Wherever fishermen gather there will be talk of gear: of what works, what's new and what they consider junk. There are new techniques, new equipment and new places to try, but of course these are only mentioned after they have stopped producing. How to deal with stray electricity in a boat not properly grounded or with marauding sea lions are popular topics. But before any of this information is taken as fact, it must be weighed. Who is the source? Does he actually catch fish, and who is he talking to?

Most fishermen are caught between wanting to share solitary triumphant moments and protecting the knowledge which brings them success. A big part of fishing is the competition so, perched along gunwales and seated on hatch covers they gather, and in a tight-lipped way let out only so much as will make a good story. For the keen listener who can sort the hot tips from the bull, there can be some valuable information.

AYE AYE on the rocks. (COLLECTION OF JAE PROCTOR)

Billy absorbed these stories. One highliner who sold to Jae, John Kallas on *Gurd*, took a special interest in the boy and took him under his wing. He told Billy to polish his spoons and *always* keep his hooks sharp. A fisherman since 1919, Kallas knew what he was talking about and he became the boy's mentor and idol. From the time he was little, Billy had watched the man craft his spoons, believing that if he could make spoons as good, he had a chance of becoming a highliner himself.

A store-bought spoon cost 35¢, so most people made their own. Kallas showed Billy how to cut a 75¢-sheet of brass into a dozen spoons. He gave Billy a yew-wood mould, with shallow depressions carved in it, and a little brass hammer, and taught him how to hammer out his own spoons.

To work properly, a spoon must be bent perfectly and be of the correct size, shape and colour. The idea is to mimic something a salmon is most attracted to — a wounded herring. Herring are a preferred prey for salmon, and a wounded one is an easy meal. A well-made spoon swims along with a wobble. Kallas tested and reworked each new spoon until it moved just the way he wanted it to. Of course, everyone has a slightly different opinion of what "just right" is. Success depends on thinking like a fish.

Kallas checked each newly made spoon, attaching it to a short line off the end of a ten-foot pole. Then he trotted along the dock and watched its action in the water. If the spoon spun or vibrated erratically, too fast or too slow, a few more taps of the hammer were needed to make it sashay along perfectly. Kallas boasted that once, while he was testing a perfect new spoon, a big spring appeared from under the float with a herring in its mouth. Kallas claimed that when the salmon spied his shiny spoon wobbling along, it spat out the herring and grabbed the spoon. This was the ultimate approval of his handiwork.

There were many kind fishermen offering Billy advice and encouragement in the early days of his commercial fishing. Albert "No Talk" Hudson was a man of few words, but he liked Billy and Billy hung on everything Albert had to say about fishing.

Bill Sinclair was a well-known fisherman who knew the coast from Washington to Alaska. He recorded his adventures in poems, and books like *Poor Man's Rock*, about handtrolling in the Gulf of Georgia. His boat, *Who Who*, had a big owl painted on the riding sail. He was one of the first to fish the banks north of Port Hardy and he had the first autopilot Billy ever saw. It was a 1946 Wood Freeman, powered by two dry-cell batteries; Sinclair called it his "Iron Mike."

Spoon-making mould and hammer given to Billy by John Kallas. (PHOTO BY ALEXANDRA MORTON)

Miles "Whitey" Wint on *MW* was a generous man who gave freely of his time when someone needed help. One night, as Billy came in on *Aye Aye*, a valve stuck on the Easthope. Billy had to take the head off and grind it down a bit. Old Whitey was there to help. Billy planned to leave it till the next morning, but Whitey insisted, "No, we'll do it tonight so you can fish in the morning." Another time, when the stern bearing wore out, Billy put the boat on the grid and set to work on it at the 8:00 AM low tide. Whitey stayed for the day to help. Billy has never forgotten the good will and generosity freely offered by these men.

The worst mess I ever got into while fishing was the first year I had *Aye Aye*. I was spring fishing at Flower Island and I was playing a big spring. I never took the snap off the cable and the break on the gurdy let go with a 35-pound lead on the end. The line went flying. It tore the hook out of the spring and the hook went into the ball of my thumb. My arm was dragged over the side by the weight. I couldn't reach the leader with my other hand to pull it up because I would have fallen overboard and I couldn't reach the gurdy to put it in gear and pull up the weight. Well, I had to just hang there while the hook slowly tore out of my thumb. After that I always undid the snap from the line.

★★★

Some people yearn to travel. They long to escape the known and experience something different. Others are born to the right place and love their home deeply throughout their lives. Billy Proctor falls into the second category. In 1947, Jae decided she could afford a trip to Vancouver with her good friend Mrs. Kimbles, the wife of a logger, who lived in Farewell Harbour. They booked passage on the Union Steamship *Cardena* and headed south after the fishing season.

The ships were often overcrowded and overloaded, but they were fun, and Billy enjoyed the first leg of the journey. They had a little cabin and he listened for the sound of the steward's xylophone announcing the different meal sittings. The food was wonderful and, served on crisp, linen tablecloths with silverware, it all looked very splendid.

There was the punchboard to be played, a form of gambling and therefore illegal. It was kept under the counter, but everyone knew it was there. A punchboard was a box with 500 little holes bored into it and a tightly rolled strip of paper in each one. For ten cents you were given a "key" and could pull out one of the paper strips. Each strip named a different prize, from cigarettes to second chances. Billy's favourite was the box of chocolates.

After the excitement of the ferry, Vancouver was anticlimactic. While riding *Lady Cecilia*, on a day trip between Vancouver and Gibson's Landing, Billy received a blast from her horn right in his ear. The ear was hurt by the extremely loud noise and a serious infection resulted. The doctor recommended that Billy's tonsils be removed so he was hospitalized for the remainder of his vacation. The cavernous halls of St. Paul's Hospital must have seemed a horribly alien environment, and being confined in a bed among strangers did not leave fond memories.

When his mum took him to Vancouver again the next year, Billy ended up back in the same hospital for three weeks with double

Billy, Jae and Mrs. Kimbles in Vancouver. (COLLECTION OF JAE PROCTOR)

pneumonia. Jae suggested another trip in 1949, but Billy opted to sit this one out. For Billy, going to the city meant only illness, doctors and St. Paul's, and he was far happier home alone.

★★★

The animal world always held great fascination for Billy. He spent hours lying on the dock watching fish. Occasionally, he was able to observe halibut sucking food in and out several times before swallowing it. He knew one eagle from her birth.

I got to know this eagle real well because she lived on Swanson Island about two miles from Freshwater Bay. She was hatched in a nest on Bold Head and I first saw her in August in 1944. She was just learning to fly and I was just learning to fish so we had a bit in common. When I went trolling by the nest I would see her sitting on the edge flapping her wings. I would throw a cod over and the mother or dad would come and pick it up and take it to the nest. By the end of September she was flying around, but was real clumsy. I never went out to Bold Head after fishing season in the fall or winter, but in spring I was back fishing for bluebacks to eat. If I got a cod I would toss it out to that eagle. The first few times the young one tried, she would miss the cod and some other eagle would get it. But in a while she learned how to get them on the first try.

She was a big, handsome bird. She looked bigger than her parents, but it was just big feathers. After 3½ years she had the mature pure white head and tail, just like her parents, and one day in early spring she had a mate.

They were both sitting on the same limb, about a foot apart, talking away. I wanted to watch them more, to see where they were going to build their nest, but I had to go home or Mum would worry. I told Mum I'd like to go and see where they were going to build, and sometimes she would come too.

Well, one day, they were gone. So I looked all around Bold Head and there was no sign of them until I was on my way home. They were sitting in an old fir. The next time I went up

Big fish in Freshwater Bay. Forty-nine pounder and 54 pounder caught off Flower Island in 1950. Billy, Julia Eckoff. (PHOTO BY JAE PROCTOR)

there they had started to build a nest. It was a good spot for fish, lots of tide, and it was a good lookout spot. The big fir was about six feet across and over a hundred feet tall. It had a big flat top and big strong limbs.

Soon they had the nest done, the eggs were in it and they were taking turns sitting on them. Whenever I went trolling by, I would save any little cod and toss it to them. One of the pair would come and get it. If there was just one in the nest it would call and call and the other one would come and get the cod and take it to the nest. Then they would sit and talk it over.

Every year they raised one or two babies. One year some loggers came and started to log near the nest. They were falling trees all around and the eagles would sit and talk and talk. I often wondered what they were saying. But the loggers never fell their tree. In fact, they left a narrow strip of trees around it and the loggers left and the eagles were safe.

I was there one day when one of them went to get a fish that was too big and he went in the water and had to swim ashore with his wings. All the time he was in the water the other one was calling to him. I think the male does most of the fishing when they are nesting and I think the male goes farther afield, but I don't know for sure. One day, after 30 years, a big storm came and blew down the tree. They moved to another tree, but I never saw them build a new nest. Maybe they were too old.

Bald eagles mate for life and are very fond of each other. They can spot a fish three miles away and they love to soar in the wind. One thing I will never understand is how they know to go up Knight Inlet or Kingcome when the oolichans are spawning.

★★★

In 1947, when Billy was 13 years old, he got his first job.

This guy came and asked me if I wanted a job as a whistle punk. I said, "Sure, when do I start?" and he said, "Monday." He said he would pick me up at 7:00 AM and asked if I had any caulkboots. I said no, so he said he would bring an old pair from camp. So, 7:00 AM, I am ready and they come in the old camp boat and there are ten men. I was as shy as they come. Thank God we didn't have far to go. All the men did was swear and talk about women. They were logging up at Bold Head.

We tied to the A-frame and I put on these boots the boss gave me. I'm sure they must have been size 14 because my foot moved four inches before the boot moved. We got up the hill to where I was to be whistle punk. The hooktender is the boss out in the woods, so he was the one I took orders from. They call them hookers for short.

I will never forget that hooker. He was a mean old Finlander and he chewed snuff and spit on everything. On top of that he spoke broken English. Anyway, he showed me the whistle wire, about a thousand feet, and he showed me how to coil it around my neck in long loops so they would go down to my knees. I got it all coiled and took off. Well, you leave one end at the yarder [winch] and then you start out across the fell-and-bucked timber and you throw loops off your neck as you go.

I sure had one hell of a time that first morning. Boots that were too big and 120 pounds of wire around my neck. At last I got it all out and they started to log.

The hooker screamed, "Slack the haulback," and I just sat there. I didn't know what the hell he wanted. He screamed again, and this time he was mad. I screamed back that no one had told me what the signals were. So one of the chokermen came and sat with me for a while till I got to know what to do. He also told me that if the old hooker gave me a hard time to tell him to go f--- himself. I didn't know what it meant but I said I would remember that.

Everything went fine for a few days. Then we had a southeast gale and it was hard to hear. The hooker sounded like a raven with laryngitis. Somehow we made it through the day and on the boat going home that night, the old Finlander was giving me shit because I couldn't hear him. He asked if I was deaf and I said no, but I said, "If your mouth wasn't full of snuff you might be able to holler a bit more."

The next day was a bad day, southeast gales and sleet, and I had no raingear. So I got a fire going and I built a roof with some limbs. At about 10:00 the old hooker comes over to my fire, warms his hands and tells me they are going to move to the other side of the slash.

So I had to coil my wire around my neck all the way back to the yarder and take off across the fell-and-bucked again. I was about halfway when the old hooker started yelling to go ahead on the mainline. I just ignored him and kept going. Then he yelled again and swore at me and I yelled if he could do it any faster to come and do it himself.

I finally got to my spot and did my duty. Then I started to get cold and I could see my nice fire across the setting. But I'd be damned if I was going to start another fire. That night going home the old hooker gave me hell for being so slow. I told him I'd done my best. The chokerman's name was Paddy and he was a nice man. He got me out on deck and told me again to tell the old hooker to go f--- himself. He said it's the only thing he understands.

It went on like that for a few days and then one day I had to help pull strawline [a small line that you drag around by hand to pull a big line]. So I'm down the hill about 600 feet from my whistle and the hooker yells he had enough strawline, then right away he yells to go ahead on the strawline. I'm running as fast as I can uphill to get to the whistle and he yells again and swore at me. In order to get to my whistle I had to pass the old hooker, so just about the time I'm right alongside of him he yells a third time and I thought that's it. I walked right up to him and I said, "Why don't you go f--- yourself." He looked at me like I had hit him. He let go a big stream of snoose juice and, by God, after that we got along just fine.

Jae was a smart woman, always watching out for her business. When the 32 Nanaimo fishermen who sold to her found fish farther north and began tying up in Yokohama Bay for the night, Jae knew she had a problem. Spence Turner was sending his packer, *Mitchell Bay*, to buy their fish and this meant valuable revenue was lost for Proctor's Fish Camp. Nothing about fishing is the same from year to year. Flexibility is important and so when

Logging show on Swanson Island. Billy was 15. (PHOTO BY JAE PROCTOR)

the fishermen began to find Freshwater Bay a little too far out of their way to return to each evening, Jae decided to move.

Jae wasn't especially fond of Freshwater Bay. It held reminders of losing her little girl and her husband, and she expressed her deep sadness in poems to both of them year after year. Freshwater Bay was also a terrible anchorage in the winter. The southeast storms piled into it and, even though Billy pulled the docks up the beach after fishing each year, the storms that inevitably arrived with big tides caused damage. It was a dismal place in winter, lashed relentlessly by wind and waves. Moving seemed a good idea all around.

Bill Proctor Sr. had left the Freshwater Bay property in his son's name so when Billy was old enough to sell it, that's what they did. Harold Walden, a logger raised in Baronet Pass, bought it for $3,000, a float and the manpower to move Jae's house onto it. Proctor's was going to become a floating camp. It made good sense because it would allow them to follow the fishermen and to move to sheltered waters for the winter. Their living quarters, the store and the post office were all conveniently housed in one building, so only one structure had to be moved onto the float. The scales and fishbins were already out on the docks. Walden got Morris Cabeen, a summer fisherman/winter logger, to give him a hand with the move.

Inland, most houses stay in one place as long as they remain standing, but coastal structures are not necessarily granted this privilege. Buildings move regularly, appearing and disappearing according to their owners' needs. Houses move onto land, and onto floats, and once floating are shuffled about like furniture. The most difficult of these transitions is moving a house from the land to a float.

First and foremost, the building must be firmly seated on a substantial sled made of two logs, stiffly cross-braced. A diagonal angle is cut beneath the leading edges of these logs to allow them to slide instead of dig in. Jae's home, built in 1919 to house 50 Japanese men working at a saltery, wasn't the finest example of workmanship and it wasn't built on sled logs. The first job was getting a pair fixed into place. The back end of the 42- by 20-foot house rested on a gentle hill, while the front was raised up on posts.

Walden and Cabeen yarded two logs up the hill, placed them under the house and braced them with stout beams. Billy was assigned the task of cutting out the posts supporting the house so it would come down to rest on the sled. He took them out a slice at a time and the house lurched a little with each one he banged out. Finally, the building sat squarely on the logs and was ready for its run to the sea. This is the most dangerous part; once set in motion, a building can keep running, miss the float and dive into the water.

In March 1956, Walden placed the new float against the beach, as a very high tide was rising. On the seaward side, he tied a second float carrying a 1010 Lawrence winch. The Lawrence winch was the first gas-powered winch; the 1010 held 1,000 feet of cable and the 1012 1,200 feet. The winch cable ran across the new float and up to a harness looped around the sled logs. As Cabeen started the winch, the cables tightened and the house began ploughing deep furrows down to the beach, honeysuckle ripping from the walls. Jae stayed inside guarding her dishes. The house groaned and creaked as it inched towards the beach and the brick chimney collapsed.

The float sank in response to the weight of the building as it was eased aboard and then rose to balance when it was dragged into the

Jae's house being moved onto a float, 1956. (PHOTO BY JAE PROCTOR)

centre. Proctor's Fish Camp was seaborne. Having survived the move, Jae's home became a floathouse, a classic and distinctive coastal dwelling.

Jae never really liked life afloat. The brutish force of north-coast tides and wind were now a part of her daily existence. Everything was always moving; up and down with the tide, back and forth with the wind. Even the water in her bath tub jostled about restlessly. Perhaps if she had taken to operating boats she might have adjusted to life afloat more easily, but this was not the case. Her business, however, thrived and her son took to floathousing like a duck to water.

During summers, the Proctors moored in Yokohama Bay and as promised, the Nanaimo Gang sold to Jae. Billy, meanwhile, had become a serious contender for highliner status. In the winter months the camp was towed north into the protection of the Broughton Archipelago.

In 1956, Billy decided to try logging again so after the fishing season closed, they towed their camp to Jumble Island in Knight Inlet. They tied to Hank Alonzo Roth's logging outfit and Billy went to work for him. Roth was a hard-working man who had made his way to the coast from the family homestead in Missouri.

When Hank Roth's father had first viewed the Missouri land he planned to settle on, it had looked good and he made the purchase for three dollars an acre. But when he returned with his family, he was very disappointed to find that much of the property had become a lake. Undaunted, he set one son to trapping the muskrat which populated their lake, selling the pelts for seven cents apiece. The rest of the family farmed and ran a dry-goods business. Hank was expected to manage the store, but he hated being imprisoned inside. He needed to be outdoors and the wilder the territory, the better, so Hank got a team of horses and headed north where he bought fish from a river fishery for two cents per pound. He hauled them 200 miles by sled, sold them for eight to ten cents per pound and figured it was well worth the effort.

In time, Hank made his way to the coast and began logging in Fife Sound. He recalled the "hungry thirties" as his happiest years. "Everyone was equal," he stated and despite the hard times on the coast, "Only one guy was on welfare." There were dances once a month in the schoolhouse or in the bunkhouses at the old shingle-bolt mill up in Echo Bay, and picnics that lasted all day and on through the night. There was enough work and good times to keep everyone happy. Roth's camp was a friendly place.

Percy Macleod was the powder man who worked for Hank Roth, handling all the explosives. Hank had a big floathouse with an outhouse on one end. Under the outhouse there was a long log that stuck out farther than the rest of the float-logs and everything that dropped down from the outhouse collected on it. Percy noticed this and one day he went to Hank and said he could cut that log off with dynamite. Since the log was underwater, a saw couldn't be used, so Hank agreed.

Percy got under the house, put a string of dynamite around the log and lit the fuse. Hank's wife, Margaret, was in the house at the time of the blast. Their house was lined with V-jointed cedar planks and when the dynamite went off, the V-joints came apart. Margaret thought the entire house was going to collapse. Percy succeeded in cutting the log under the outhouse, but now Hank had to redo the interior of his house.

Hank Roth's floating camp in Yokohama Bay, Swanson Island, 1957. (PHOTO BY BILLY PROCTOR)

Hank gave his newest employee the treacherous job of falling old fir snags on Midsummer Island. When a cut was made into those ancient, dead giants, Billy never knew if the tree would hold together or break apart, coming down in chunks on his head. Billy figured, "The old fart was trying to get rid of me, but I was lucky."

After three weeks of that, Billy did a lot more falling for Hank. He liked the job. It was clean work and there was no one to boss him around. He started with a Super Twin IEL chainsaw with a 60-inch bar, weighing about a hundred pounds. When no one was around, Billy would start up the saw at the bottom of the hillside, put the bar to the ground and let the saw pull him up the hill. Hank would take Billy over to Midsummer Island at 7:00 AM, drop him off on the beach and return to pick him up at 5:00 PM. This left Billy with no way to get back to camp in case of an accident. When he cut his knee with an axe, he went down to the A-frame float and rummaged around for a bandage. He found a forgotten lunch box with some bandage material stowed in it, wrapped his knee in cloth and went back up the hill to work. There was no first-aid attendant.

I was 21 years old when I went to fall snags for Hank Roth. I'd been working in logging camps off and on since 1947, but I had always come home at night, so I always ate at home.

I will never forget that first morning. There was a bowl of boiled eggs on the table and up till then I had never eaten a boiled egg without an egg cup. I was real hungry, but I didn't know what to do with them so I just sat there and waited to see how the other men dealt with the eggs and then did the same.

And at home the only thing I drank was Toddy which was like hot chocolate, or else I drank Ovaltine which was much the same. Well, in the cookhouse there was coffee and tea. I took a cup of coffee and never put any sugar or milk in it and I took a big gulp. I thought I'd been poisoned.

In March of 1956 Billy met the boss's daughter. Yvonne Murial Gladys Roth was a very independent, slender blonde and she caught Billy's attention immediately.

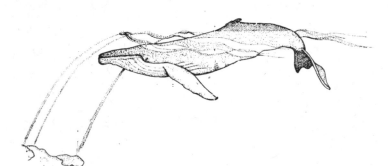

Chapter Four

I've learned to do my washing
In an old five gallon can,
And I've learned that beans and bacon
Can fill a hungry man.

A TRUE MAINLANDER, Yvonne Roth was born in a floathouse in one of the most remote bodies of water on the coast, Nepah Lagoon. What makes Nepah remote is not how far up the coast it lies, but the entrance, which can only be navigated twice a day. The long, narrow lagoon tapers down to a tight bottleneck at the southern end. When the tide is falling, the water can't flow out fast enough and as a result the water level inside the lagoon becomes higher than sea level.

The opposite occurs when the tide is flooding in and the lagoon can't fill fast enough. The seething waters actually form a type of waterfall, called an overfall, and it is not a good place for a boat to be. For a few minutes twice a day the water levels inside the lagoon and outside are the same, and the hellish passage calms before reversing direction. A skipper must time his passage to arrive at that moment.

Every two or three years Hank Roth moved his floating camp to start logging a new claim. The camp included bunkhouses, a cookhouse, his home and assorted sheds, each on a separate float. Instead of seeking sheltered waters, like most people tying up floathouses, Hank simply tied the floats as close as possible to the lease. His daughter surmised that he took pride in tying up to rough, exposed shorelines. Waves broke over their front deck, paintings never hung straight for long and the house creaked and moaned like an old sailing ship.

Hank happened to be near Echo Bay when Yvonne, the youngest child, was ready to start school, so she attended the one-room school with her brother Johnny and sister Margaret. When she was in grade two, however, it was time to move to another claim and the children began correspondence lessons. Hank was a strong believer in correspondence schooling, convinced that it forced children to become good writers. He was never concerned that his nomadic ways deprived his children of a good education.

Yvonne loved her coastal home. Overly confident, she too had no use for a life jacket. The one time she was pressed into wearing one, she had no idea how it worked and put it on upside down. On occasion, her mother tied a loop of gillnet corks around each child before the threesome scampered out onto the floating logs corralled in a boom alongside the camp. This was a dangerous playground.

Cedar and fir logs, large and buoyant, barely moved when the children alighted, but these were not the logs they were interested in. What they sought were the hemlocks, low in the water with very little buoyancy. The children could sink a small hemlock by standing on one end. When they were up to their armpits in the bone-chilling water, they sprang to the next log. If they had slipped and gone under the water, the tightly boomed logs would have sealed the surface.

Yvonne never learned to swim, despite frequent "lessons." With a rope tied around her waist, she was repeatedly tossed into the sea to sink or swim. Some people float naturally and others don't. Poor "Buckshot," as she was called, was a definite sinker and the lessons didn't help.

The young Roths were off exploring and fishing in their rowboats from an early age. They enjoyed poking and prowling about the shoreline and were avid fishermen. As the children caught rock cod and sole, they plopped them into a submerged box tied to the float. This "livebox" was a loosely built wooden crate with a lid, kept submerged so the fish could live in it, until they became dinner.

When the camp was tied to the bluffs in Fife Sound, Yvonne and Johnny were surprised by two humpback whales. One enormous whale surfaced on each side of the tiny rowboat, their breath exploding into the quiet morning. The loggers on the float screamed for the startled children to *rowww!* Johnny, who was standing when the whales blew, grabbed at the oars and began

Children are still attracted to booms. Darien Berry playing on logs in front of the Proctors' homestead. (PHOTO BY ALEXANDRA MORTON)

Humpback whales in Knight Inlet. (PHOTO BY ALEXANDRA MORTON)

rowing frantically, but his oars never touched the water. Scared at first, Yvonne doubled over in a fit of laughter, and the memory still brings a smile to her face.

Yvonne recalls watching humpback whales in their boom. The floating logs would begin to stir and buckle as a whale pushed straight up until a huge knobby face parted the logs in a whale spyhop. They were probably scratching themselves, the rough bark of the tightly packed logs reaching hard-to-get-at places in a satisfying way.

A mature humpback can reach a length of 60 feet, and although quite huge, they pose no threat to people. The only dangerous incident involving a humpback was in the floating community at Sullivan Bay. Skimming along the surface, feeding, the unfortunate creature caught a boomchain in its open mouth. The whale seemed unable to swim backward to free itself and thrashed about, half under the float and in danger of drowning. A brave soul roped it by the tail and dragged it out backward, saving both the float and the whale.

The humpback whale that lived in Fife Sound was well known. A large barnacle sat squarely on its back so the whale became known as "Barney." Often, Barney was accompanied by a second whale, which became "The Missus." Barney and The Missus sometimes fed in Viner Sound and it was there they were sighted by a woman who, out of ignorance and fear, did not want whales around. She decided to get rid of them by calling the Coal Harbour Whaling Station. In 1952, there were the two humpbacks in Fife Sound, another six in Knight Inlet, several more in Kingcome Inlet and, of course, Joe at Freshwater Bay.

Two whalers and a towboat, *Nahmint*, responded to the call.

I'll never forget that day in August. I was trolling in the mouth of Knight Inlet and I saw the old *Nahmint* coming out, towing all the old whales alongside. I just about cried and that was the last of the humpbacks in the Mainland for many years. Now we just see the odd one pass by. I used to think a lot about old Joe and Barney who had grown to trust humans and then got shot by a human. Life is like that sometimes. It was never the same without old Joe puffing along the kelp beds of Flower Island waiting for slack tide.

★★★

When Yvonne's family was tied in Mackenzie Sound they went berry picking on Sundays; Hank didn't log on Sundays. Yvonne loved those outings more than anything else. They had to climb quite a distance, but the reward was the best berry of all, the blue huckleberry. Blue huckleberries grow at higher elevations than the red variety, but are well worth the climb. Bears were busy looking for berries too and their fermented berry breath hung heavily in the still, morning air. Yvonne and Margaret argued constantly as they hiked and often found themselves far ahead in heated debate. Their raised voices were enough to keep the bears out of their path, but the many porcupines were either somewhat deaf, or didn't care, because the girls encountered them frequently.

When buckets and bellies were full, they headed home. No one had refrigerators, only "meatsafes," which were cupboards built on the outside wall of the house with many holes drilled in them. The combination of breeze and shade extended the shelf life of some foods, but not by much. The berries were quickly made into scrumptious desserts and jelly.

In 1944, Yvonne's mother decided to live in Vancouver. She wasn't leaving Hank; she was simply tired of the confines of floathouse living and the waves across her front porch. Before she went, Mrs. Roth insisted she have the final say about who cooked at her husband's camp; Yvonne remembers every cook had remarkably similar stout figures. Mrs. Roth and her children entered a different world, catering banquets at the Regent Palace Hotel and running a boarding house. The children were enrolled at Lord Roberts School.

Yvonne despised her new life and her school. Used to doing schoolwork at home with just her brother and sister, she was now in the biggest crowd of children she had ever seen. Worse, she had nothing in common with them. They were city kids and she was from the wilderness. They had no experience with Yvonne's world, didn't know what she was talking about, and teased the strange new girl relentlessly. When Yvonne tried to describe her dad's logging operation and mentioned the winches called "donkeys," they poked fun at the little girl about living in the forest with a bunch of jackasses. And so it went.

One child understood Yvonne. Iris Hill had attended Echo Bay School when Yvonne was there and she knew the coast life. Her parents fished and sold their catch to Proctor's Fish Camp. Iris was Billy's good friend too. Their favourite pastime had been catching toads, and they had so many of the little amphibians penned near the creek that their "ribit, ribits" kept Jae awake. Iris became a friend to both the isolated boy and the small girl lost among strangers.

When she was 17, Yvonne got a job at the St. Regis Paper Factory, making bags for cement and sugar. Starting wages were 52¢ an hour, but soon a union was formed and her pay jumped to $1.75 per hour. Yvonne chose to work the night shift, from 4:00 PM to midnight, because it gave her more freedom during the day. The drawback was travelling the dark streets home every night. She had it carefully choreographed. If she left the factory promptly, she

Steam donkey raising an A-frame, for Richardson and Heywood's logging operation, Yokohama Bay, 1935. (PHOTO BY JAE PROCTOR)

could catch a streetcar which connected almost immediately with a bus. When she got off the bus she ran as fast as she could, down the centre of the street, until she reached her home. Yvonne had never been afraid of the dark inlets or forest trails, but half-lit city streets were terrifying.

The Vancouver Brewery, with their draft horses, and a nearby tire factory brought the smells of hops, manure, and tar into the paper factory. In the constant haze of dust, the odours blended into a unique stench. The work was sheer drudgery, but Yvonne made good friends and went on trips with them, as far as Hollywood. Yvonne planned to work ten years at St. Regis, but when her doctor examined her lungs and found pleurisy, he told her to get out of the dust before it killed her. Yvonne noticed many co-workers had breathing problems, even tuberculosis. So, two years before she was to receive the coveted gold pin for service, she headed back north.

Yvonne had planned a couple of idle vacation months at her father's camp. Hank, however, had other ideas. When Yvonne arrived, he informed her that she was the cook and would "blow whistles," for 50¢ a day! This didn't come as a big surprise. Johnny and Margaret had held these positions before her and Johnny was still there. Hank didn't pay all of his employees so poorly, only family. "We all work together and everything goes into the pot," were familiar words. He also held that "charity begins at home," and borrowed $200 that Yvonne had saved, to buy supplies for his camp. He was prodded into repaying it only after Mrs. Roth had a few words with him.

Yvonne worked as whistle punk, Johnny choked the logs (wrapped a cable around each one so it could be pulled), Hank operated the donkey and Billy unhooked the logs. First the trees were felled and pulled out of the woods. There was no need to limb them as the branches tore off when the trees were dragged to the spar tree (a tall pole erected with a pulley at the top) and laid carefully in a "cold deck pile." The formation of this pile was something of an art as it often grew to a thousand logs. It had to be stacked so that each log could be taken off without destroying the pile. One fellow mistakenly hooked a key log, and as it moved, the entire pile collapsed. When he saw the mess he'd made, he walked off the job and never returned. Hank was left with an over-sized, life-threatening game of pick-up sticks.

After all the logs reached the spar tree the rigging was changed and each log was dragged from the cold deck pile to the water. Hank, who was down on the float with the winch, couldn't see Johnny up in the bush choking the logs, so they both relied on Yvonne for communication. One whistle meant "Stop." It also meant "Go Ahead." This caused mix-ups if someone lost track of the sequence of things. Two blasts followed by four signalled that Hank should slack the haulback line and six quick toots meant slack the mainline. Seven blasts meant an injury. Yvonne was seated back in the woods, and at times couldn't see her brother due to the thick brush, so she had to listen for his commands. The ravens, however, sometimes imitated Johnny's repetitive shouts. They were known for this behaviour all over the coast, and Yvonne was never sure if it was Johnny or a raven. When in doubt, all she had to do was wait a minute for the follow-up scream of impatience to clear things up.

Yvonne loved being back up the coast. It was cold out on the wet, misty hillsides, but she was breathing clean air again and it

Cold deck pile at spar tree, ready to be dragged into the water. Hank Roth's operation, 1930s. (COLLECTION OF JAE PROCTOR)

smelled sweet after the factory. Some days she built a small fire under a log and sat with her feet dangling over it. She was home.

★★★

In 1957, six months after meeting Yvonne, Billy pored over the Acme catalogue, looking at engagement rings. When he proposed, he was ready with ring in hand. She accepted, and on the last day their marriage licence was valid they took the leap.

Billy and Yvonne spent their honeymoon on beautiful little Loose Lake above Scott Cove. They built a raft and paddled with boards across to the far end, fishing for trout as they went. When a west wind came up, it took them five hours to paddle the half-sunk raft back to their camp. But they didn't care. They were two hard-working, young people in love, and on one of the few vacations either had ever taken.

Billy and Yvonne's married life began without a home. They lived part time on Billy's boat and part time at Hank's camp. As soon as Billy found an affordable floathouse, he bought it, and with

Yvonne and Billy's wedding day, 1957. (PHOTO BY JAE PROCTOR)

Darrel Brown's help, towed it from Richmond Bay in Drury Inlet to Insect Island, where Jae's house was tied. Southeast winds of 70 knots began to blow as they set out. It would have been easier to wait out the blow, but half the fun was not knowing for sure if they'd make it. The little house was wet and salty clear to the roof peak and had slid around considerably on the float, but it survived the trip. The outhouse, however, had been lost overboard.

It was probably a good thing that neither Yvonne nor Billy owned a stick of furniture, because there was no place to put it. The house was so small, with a built-in bed and breakfast nook, and a stove, that there wasn't even room for a chair. The leaky roof, which was not improved by the wild ride from Drury Inlet, played a tune every rainy night, "Plink, plunk, plop, splat." Jars and bottles were strategically placed to catch the drips. There was no indoor plumbing and since the outhouse had fallen off, they ran the slippery float-logs to use Jae's facilities. Despite it all, Billy and Yvonne loved their new home. It was warm and had the cosy breakfast nook where they lingered over Yvonne's good cooking.

A beautiful, ornate oil stove kept their little house dry and cooked their meals. Some oil stoves burn cleanly, but others produce daily crops of soot which hang from the insides of the pipes and cooking surface. When enough collects, the stove is starved for oxygen and the flame goes out in a spawn of tiny, velvety, soot balls from every crack. These black bubbles defy gravity, drifting great distances before finally coming to rest with a black, greasy smudge. Yvonne's stove produced soot prolifically and needed to be cleaned almost daily. Most of her first year of marriage Yvonne was covered with the smeary black powder.

Billy was worse than no help at all. In an over-zealous moment he decided to surprise his wife with a shot to the chimney. Unfortunately, Yvonne was cleaning, with her head in the stove. As the bullet struck the pipe, soot exploded downwards, blackening not only Yvonne, but her entire home as well. The once-blonde woman emerged black and proceeded to paint the air blue. Billy was not a popular guy that day. Irrepressible, Billy also delighted in setting off small explosions in her flower boxes.

Dynamite was readily available because it was used in logging in a variety of ways. One of the biggest problems with log floats are teredos, a type of marine worm that eats wood. As they eat, they bore holes in logs, consuming everything except the knots. Logs can be so attractive to these worms that after only a few years, the knots stick out eight inches or more, all the surrounding wood having been chewed away. The less wood there is on a log, the less buoyant it becomes until it begins to sink. One way of getting rid of teredos was a ¾ stick of stumping powder. Home owners put it in a can with a 50-foot fuse and then slid the can under the float. Once positioned, the fuse was lit and *boom!* The worms died of shock. Too much powder, of course, rattled the houses on the float apart.

Dynamite was occasionally used for fishing as well. To catch herring, half a stick of stumping powder was put in a can with a cap and long fuse. The can was lowered on a string to the right depth, tied off to a bobber and the fuse lit. It was essential that the fisherman leave the arèa as quickly as possible after the fuse was lit. Following a blast, the stunned herring were easy to pick up.

With this technique in mind, Alan Brown from Shawl Bay and a friend set out in a little boat to get some herring for halibut bait. They dropped the can overboard and lit the fuse, but when they put the motor in gear, it stalled. Despite frantic cranking, it refused to restart. The float tied to the can of stumping powder was bobbing against their hull, bubbles from the burning fuse coming up under the stern. When Alan noticed the bubbles, the men dove for the bow just as the powder went off. The boat's stern flew six feet up in the air and came down with such force it knocked the caulking out from between the planks. Water started coming in all over. The destructive fishing technique almost destroyed the fishermen.

Fred Buzzard used dynamite in an imaginative way. Fred was attracted to the coast when he was still a lad. At first he worked as a trapper for a man who had a trapline in Mackenzie Sound. Fred was dropped off with food and traps and picked up in six weeks. Then he became a logger. When he started logging he sometimes used spar trees in addition to an A-frame. One spar tree Fred chose in Thompson Sound was too dangerous to top by hand, because it had several tops. Undaunted, Fred cut a notch all the way around the top of the tree where he wanted to fall it and put a row of dynamite in the notch. Then he fixed two blasting caps in place where they could be seen from the ground.

The next morning he took his rifle to work. The young lad he had working as whistle punk asked Fred what he was planning to shoot. He replied that he was going to shoot the top right off the spar tree. When they got near the tree Fred found a good spot to rest the barrel of the rifle, took aim and shot the blasting cap. The top of the tree just lifted off and fell over. The kid had no idea dynamite had been involved and talked for years about what a hell of a shot Fred Buzzard was.

In 1959, Blackfish Sound was closed to fishing for a week, because the fish stocks were declining — the first time it had ever been closed. Billy could see that to continue fishing in years ahead he was going to have to go west. The few men working the open waters west of Vancouver Island were making excellent catches, so in the same year he got married, Billy sold *Aye Aye* for $2,200 and took on a major debt to buy *Fisher Boy*. The price was $10,000 and he borrowed $7,200 at 7½% interest from Alert Bay Shipyards. *Fisher Boy* was a big boat, 43 feet long with a ten-foot beam. Billy was sure he would pay it off quickly with big catches west of Port Hardy. However, *Fisher Boy* was a problem from day one and Billy concedes today that the boat was his biggest mistake.

On a trip to Alert Bay shortly after the purchase, the oil pump failed, and Billy and Yvonne found themselves adrift. They put out a call for assistance, but it was May 24th, Queen Victoria Day, a holiday. The only boat to respond was the police boat en route to a boat parade along the waterfront of Alert Bay. Dutifully, she swung off course and picked up *Fisher Boy*.

The police boat looked splendid, freshly scrubbed, flags snapping in the breeze, but the young Proctors were only half amused at their end of the towline, with the whole town watching. Even worse, the boat needed more money sunk into repairing the oil pump. It was halibut season and the halibut boats had top priority at Alert Bay Shipyard, so Billy sat tied to the dock for 17 days waiting for his turn.

Fisher Boy gave Jae an embarrassing moment as well. She was standing on the boat one morning as Billy worked on the gurdies.

FISHER BOY. (COLLECTION OF JAE PROCTOR)

The gurdy shaft was turning and on the end was a little set screw. As Jae talked to her son, a small breeze blew her skirt against the set screw and the turning shaft wound her skirt right off.

"Poor old Mum," Billy chuckles. "We laughed about that for a long time."

When the salmon season opened, Billy and *Fisher Boy* were ready. Alone, with no deckhand, he headed for Bull Harbour at the north end of Goletas Channel. There, he took on ice and headed for Nahwitti Bar.

Wherever a narrow channel meets open water, tide and wind cause problems, but if the channel is shallow, the problems multiply. As the ocean swells meet the rising sea floor they "feel bottom" and their undersides are peeled away and sent back out to sea. Of course, that water doesn't want to go back out to sea; it has a tide to meet and come hell *and* high water it's going to do just that. As a result, the water over Nahwitti Bar forms steep, dangerously turbulent seas. The hundreds of fishermen who venture over the bar annually try to time their crossings to meet the flood tide instead of the ebb. Many skirt the edges and run through the kelp.

Fisher Boy had a successful crossing over Nahwitti Bar, but as soon as the boat began to rise and fall to the rhythm of the Pacific swell, seasickness hit Billy hard. For eight days he really didn't care if he lived or died. Deeply disappointed with his constitution, he had to get out of that swell. His hopes of repaying the loan that year were lost and *Fisher Boy* was dubbed "the pukeboat." Although Billy knew the boat was too expensive to run to make money in the inside waters, he managed $4,500 that season.

Like all highliners, Billy pays close attention to details: the colour of the water, the stage of the tide, the date, and the weather. He gradually figured out where to be when the tide was flooding and where to fish each slack tide, and he was getting a feel for how fish move. Salmon don't travel in straight lines; they sway with currents, rest behind peninsulas, zig-zag to pick up the scent of their home rivers flooding after a heavy rainfall. While a good fisherman needs to persist, he also has to experiment. The tricky part is learning when to switch gear, when to pick up and run and when to "wear a groove in the hot tack," going back and forth over the same spot for hours.

Fisher Boy at Jae's floathouse, Yokohama Bay, 1956. (Photo by Jae Proctor)

One evening, Billy returned to camp smugly triumphant. His boat was loaded with all species of salmon while the others had had a poor day. Even the legendary Nanaimo Gang, who were still on top, didn't have much to show for the day's effort. When Billy began flinging fish after fish onto the scales, keen interest lit in their eyes.

"Where the hell you been, Proctor, didn't see a sign of you all day," they asked, knowing full well a straight answer wasn't going to follow. This was all part of the game and Billy just grinned.

The next morning he didn't rev his engine, but idled out quietly before the rest were awake. By the time the others got up, Billy had disappeared. That evening he returned with another impressive load. This was more than could be ignored. The "Gang" decided to split up and track the kid down.

It was Mike Ward on *Ethel June* who spotted Billy bobbing about in the tide rips off West Cracroft Point the next afternoon. Without altering his gear, Ward pointed his bow toward *Fisher Boy* in hopes of loading up with fish. Instead, the tide grabbed *Ethel June* and took her sideways out into Johnstone Strait, making an awful mess of the "pigs." The pigs are rectangular floats snapped onto the trolling cables. These floats carry the lines back away from the boat, separating the gear so it doesn't tangle. Strong tides, however, can bring the pigs together, resulting in 20 or more hooks and flashers instantly tangled in a tight snarl. Ward never even reached Billy.

A "pig" being snapped into place on a trolling cable. (PHOTO BY JARRET MORTON)

"By Jesus," he yelled, that evening. "I found you, Proctor, but it didn't do *me* any good. You can have that gol' darn rip."

What Ward didn't know was that Billy had prepared his gear before entering the rips. He'd brought in the back pigs and was fishing only the four shorter lines which he pulled carefully in and out past the other gear. Because he had less cable out, the swirling current didn't tangle the lines.

Sockeye, with its deep red flesh, has always been highly valued. To many consumers sockeye is the *only* salmon. Its flavour is rich, but it is probably the colour that gives it its reputation. The crimson "salmon-pink" shade comes from the rosy- coloured krill of the North Pacific that these fish feed on. Of the five species of salmon, sockeye migrate the farthest out in the North Pacific. They are one of the most prolific salmon, surviving even the uncontrolled slaughter at the turn of the century in the Fraser River.

Traditionally, sockeye were considered a net fish, meaning that while seine boats and gillnetters could catch them, the trollers couldn't. Sockeye just wouldn't bite. This was a source of frustration for the troll fleet because on the big return years for the

Adams and Fraser rivers, these beautiful fish flowed beneath their hulls by the millions, untouched. When Billy came in one day with 25 aboard, that was considered a big catch.

Most salmon are attracted to small fish and the trollers had figured out how to simulate those. However, sockeye were not attracted to fish. Instead, fishermen found only the remains of small, pink krill in sockeye bellies. So, in an effort to get them to strike, all shades and types of pink material were shredded, snipped and dragged around on the end of a line. Billy cut up his hated red life jacket for bait, finally getting some use out of it. Fluorescent red wool from paratrooper uniforms, called gantren, was tried as well.

Then in 1958, Scott Plastics came out with the first red hootchies and revolutionized sockeye fishing for the trollers. A hootchie is a piece of rubbery plastic shaped to resemble a tiny octopus. The fishing line runs down through the head, a bead or two is threaded and then the hook is tied so that it is hidden within the tentacles. Known also as Dizzy Dots and Flasher Flickers, these lures were at last something sockeye were interested in and they snapped hungrily at them. In August 1958, Ellis

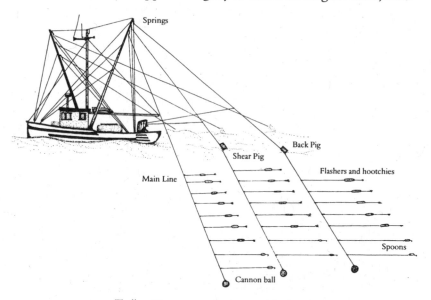

Troller. (Drawing by Alexandra Morton)

Mornay on *Kath-ell* had his picture in the paper when he landed an astronomical 500 sockeye in one day in Blackfish Sound. Not a bad day's catch even today.

Still, sockeye are a challenging fish to attract. They have to be thought of as a school rather than as individuals. To catch spring salmon, hooks are dragged slowly through rock piles. Coho are attracted to fast-moving lures near the surface and pinks bite most things going in any direction. Sockeye, however, like lots of gear, all tied exactly the same and they will often bite only while the boat is moving in one direction. Two boats can be fishing side by side and one will be loading up, while the other is getting nothing. Sometimes, a boat travelling south along a tack will produce sockeye but when it turns around, all that comes aboard are pinks. A boat pulling sockeye may lose the school to another troller that comes close enough. The school acts as one organism and you've either got its attention or you don't.

Once a boat gets going with a school, sockeye bite like nothing else. Every hook rises to the surface with a fish. The lovely green backs (or blue if they were spawned in the Fraser River) appear out of the depths one after another. Often, schoolmates will accompany a hooked fish, dropping down the line to swim with each fish before it is pulled aboard. It seems strange that the hooked fish issue no warnings.

For anyone whose survival depends on fishing, a good day on sockeye is a thrilling sight; it's as good as cash flying into the boat. Every movement must be pared down to the most simple and effective. Gracefully, the silvery fish and pink flashers come aboard in shimmering arcs. The cleaning knife must fly — rip, zip, splut — and the air bladder floats the guts into a cloud of sea gulls.

Sockeye Fever

Have you ever had sockeye fever? I think all salmon fishers have had it at one time or another in their lives. It makes you do all sorts of strange things; it is like a gold rush.

When the sockeye start to bite it's a real rush and when you see them in the water behind a flasher, just gliding along so effortlessly, it sure is a beautiful sight. I have fished more years than I want to remember and I still get excited when the bite is on.

I can be fishing springs and coho, doing not bad, when someone comes on the phone and says sockeye is going to open and all hell breaks loose. Up comes the gear and I get rid of the springs and coho at the cannery. I get new ice and go for the sockeye.

Where to go? Top Knot or Pine Island? I'll go to Top Knot and give it a try; it's not so hot there, so I go to The Lagoon and it's a little better, but still not good.

So I try Pine Island and have one good day and then too many boats show, but that's all part of sockeye fever. We get our share and they close us down till they do a count.

Some say we got too many, some say we didn't get our share, I say we'll get more in Blackfish Sound. They say I'm wrong, but in the end we go down to Blackfish Sound and fish at Bold Head and down in the pass.

Dear old Blackfish Sound is noted for its thick fog and it sure was thick this year. But there were not too many boats and so it wasn't too bad. We got a few bad tangles in the tide rips, but we got lucky most of the time. Lots of tugs and barges and big ocean liners to watch out for on the radar, but we don't worry about them when we've got sockeye fever!

We get all tangled and curse and swear, but then we get a few sockeye and we forget all about everything else. We wonder why one side of the boat is catching fish and the other side is not so I clean the grounding wire that runs between the gurdies and that seems to help. Why do fish stop biting?

Sometimes I think it has to do with B.O. [body odour]. Some mornings I forget to turn on the black box [which regulates the volts of electricity a boat releases into the water], some mornings I forget to turn off the running lights. Some fishers say you have to use green flashers, some say blue, some say red, but when you get the bite going I don't think it matters a damn.

The main thing is to get those lines clean and back in the water as fast as you can. Some guys sit in the wheelhouse and complain on the phone for an hour at a time and then wonder at the end of the day why some have more sockeye than they do.

Landing a big sockeye. (PHOTO BY ALEXANDRA MORTON)

Well, it's all over now so we will just have to wait till next year so we can do it all again. *Hey!* Sockeye on the main, *yahoo!* Sockeye on the shear pig! Sockeye on the back pig, *yahoo!* The bite is on. *Sockeye fever hits again!*

★★★

Yvonne helped her mother-in-law buy fish. While the men unloaded the boats themselves, Yvonne lifted every fish onto the scale and Jae read the weights from a little desk behind the scale. Once, while Yvonne was tossing a pink salmon, often called slime balls for obvious reasons, the fish slipped out of her hands and hit her mother-in-law in the back of her head. This did not help the already strained relationship between the two women.

Yvonne rarely got off the float to fish with her husband, but the times she did were often eventful. The day after celebrating Bud Brown's birthday into the wee hours, Yvonne found herself at the wheel of *Fisher Boy* in the wide open waters of Queen Charlotte Strait. Billy was asleep in the bunk below. Queen Charlotte Strait is a deep, expansive body of water, with only a few, widely spaced islands breaking the surface. It is a "fishy" place because it is the entrance to the passages east of Vancouver Island. Millions of salmon flow through en route to their rivers.

Each of the six lines of a troller is attached to the huge poles by a metal spring. These springs give the lines some play so a big fish is less likely to break the line. The springs also signal when there is a fish on the line. Trollers are forever craning their necks back and forth to peer at the springs. They aren't easy to read. Wavelets make them jiggle, debris gives them an erratic twitch. On a slow day a troller studies one set of springs and then twists his or her neck to look at the other set, giving these fishermen their nickname, "Swivel Necks."

On this day Yvonne was trying to read the springs as Billy slept. When one began to tug, she yelled happily, "Billy, we've got something."

Then the entire pole picked up the rhythm and started to leap around. Yvonne cried, "Billy, oh God, we've got something *big!*"

Billy flew up the companionway just in time to see the pole snap in two places. It was something big all right, as big as all of B.C. Yvonne had snagged the pinnacle seven fathoms below the surface between Foster and Holford islands, one of the few bumps in Queen Charlotte Strait.

Another time, out on "the bank," a productive piece of coastline best not named, the shaft controlling the gurdies which pull up the lines broke. Billy went to the engine room to try and rig the system back into service, but the shaft was in an awkward spot and he was having a hard time. Suddenly a big "smiley" bit, gave the springs a couple of hefty tugs and went free. (A smiley is a spring salmon weighing more than 12 pounds dressed.) Yvonne stuck her head in the cabin and yelled, "Never mind, we'll get another one," and turned the boat around to make another pass over the same spot.

Spring salmon lie along the edges of drop-offs and kelp beds; perhaps it is their sedate lifestyle that allows them to grow bigger than any other salmon. It also makes them tricky to reach. As Yvonne guided the gear toward the hot spot again, she immediately got another hit. The metal springs tugged frantically. Billy felt the

"Swivel Neck." Checking the trolling lines. (PHOTOS BY ALEXANDRA MORTON)

action and vaulted out of the engine room, but as he stepped on deck the whole boat started bouncing and he knew they'd caught a rock. Yvonne's excitement turned to horror when she realized they were anchored to a reef by their fishing hooks. What a mess. Stopping the boat to save the pole, they started pulling the tangled lines in by hand because the gurdies were still out of service. It was over an hour before they could fish again.

Things I Heard on the Floats

Going out fishing
Or is it too foggy today?
Well, maybe we could fish
In Spring Salmon Bay.

How about today?
I think it's too rough
It sure will be
Around the Bluff.

How about it now?
I think it's too calm
Wonder if the fish
Give a gol darn.

Now it's raining too hard
No, that's just right
That's the time
The fish really do bite.

It's too sunny today
The water's too clear
The fish can see
All of your gear.

I don't like to be
Tied up at the dock

So maybe I'll try it
Around the rock.

There's lots of birds
And feed in the Sound
So how about trying
The Merry-Go-Round?

The tides are too high
Or either too low
Or running too fast
Or else too slow.

Guess I'll get me
A new pair of pigs.
These ones I made
Are sure awful rigs.

Get any fish today
Around the rock?
Oh! a few lousy humps
And one old sock.

My flashers spin
Guess I'll make some more.
Wonder if they have
Any chrome in the store?

As for this new nylon
Well, it's not so hot
Mine is always breaking
Around the knot.

I lose lots of fish
I don't know why,
I blame the hooks
Too soft in the eye.

A Life Story

I tried a new hook
They said was a darb.
But mine sure ain't
They break at the barb.

Lost my best spoon
It's always the same.
Guess that's how it is
In this fishing game.

Broke my tag line
Twice to-day
Because so and so didn't
Get out of my way.

I fish six fathoms
And down 20 or more
Out in the middle
And along the shore.

I've tried brass flashers
And silver and chrome
If the fish don't come
I think I'll go home.

Look at my wires
All full of kinks
Maybe it's just me
I sure am the jinx.

My rudder rattles
My engine knocks
Even quit today
Nearly went on the rocks.

My flashers tarnish
My hooks they break

And even the fish
Won't take my bait.

I cut my bait short
I cut it long
Whatever I do
Is always wrong.

I lengthen my leaders
I figure they're right
But I have no fish
When I come in tonight.

I've tried red rubber
Pink plastic too,
Maybe next I'll try
Some yellow or blue.

I wonder if there are
Any more to come
Or are these small ones
The end of the run?

I hit it lucky
Out there today
Got quite a few coho
But the spring got away.

I got a load of humps
And some coho today
But I was fishing
Over at Double Bay.

Did you ever see
Such small fish here?
It's time the big hooknoses
Started to appear.

A Life Story

Did you see so and so?
He sure had a load!
No darn wonder...he
Never keeps the rules of the road.

He crosses your bow
Takes the shore each way
Rides your pigs
Nearly all the day.

He sure is the limit
He gets my goat
But all he says is
"My wife steers the boat."

He sure got a load
Wish they were mine!
Oh! he's using herring
I'll bet you a dime.

It's getting late
I think fishing is done.
Oh! no it ain't
There's to be another run.

Guess I'll hit the hay
It's getting late.
Oh! darn it all
I forgot to cut bait.

The packer's been
There's no fish there.
I'll give you a bit
I have some to spare.

So on and on it goes
All thru' the day

When the boats are tied
At Freshwater Bay.

I listen to their stories
Of the big fish they've caught.
Believe me, the size of them
Are bigger than I've bought!

Chapter Five

It isn't the house we live in
Nor the place in which we dwell
But the heart that beats within us
That makes our heaven or hell.

THE DEBT OWING on *Fisher Boy* made the winter of 1958-'59 a lean one for Billy and Yvonne. One night, while digging a few clams to eat, they were impressed with how easy it was to fill a sack and the idea of digging commercially was sparked. In 1958, a fishing licence cost one dollar and allowed a person to fish everything, from salmon to butter clams. Billy and Yvonne became the first non-Native people in the area to dig clams commercially and it saw them through the winter.

Every 24 hours the tide ebbs and floods twice, with one ebb lower than the other. The farther the tide goes out, the more beach is exposed for digging and because clams are generally more plentiful lower down on a beach, Billy and Yvonne wanted to be on the beach for the lowest tide of each 24-hour cycle. Unfortunately, during the winter, the lowest tides occur at night, making clam digging a bone-chilling venture. Billy and Yvonne ran through the night in their open skiff to a beach, then worked up a sweat digging and were chilled on the run to the next beach.

Eager to make as much money as possible, the Proctors dug clams on both daily low tides. They often had a thousand pounds hanging in sacks along a bluff by the time Paul Lanquist on the packer *Bonny Jane* came around to pick up the clams from all the local diggers. Since clams will stay alive in a sack for a couple of weeks, the packer arrived twice a month, timing its run to coincide with the big tides of the new and full moons. Lanquist stayed in the area for the five biggest tides, then delivered in Alert Bay. Bill Scow processed clams in Alert Bay, paying $1.60 per box. A box weighed 65 pounds and contained three fire pails worth of clams. During big tides, Billy and Yvonne dug like backhoes, averaging $25 a night.

They were a team. In the long shadows of their Coleman lantern, Billy tossed forks full of sand, broken shell and fat, squirting clams into a pile. Yvonne squatted beside the pile and sorted out the butter clams, quickly tossing them into a sack. Horse clams were flung aside and raked under before they left.

Yvonne's Clam Fritters

1 cup chopped clams
1 TBSP grated onion
1 egg, beaten
½ tsp salt
1 TBSP lemon juice
Dash of pepper
1 TBSP chopped parsley
½ cup dried bread crumbs

Mix all ingredients and drop in spoonfuls into a hot skillet.

One night, Billy was out clam digging alone in Old Pass on Baker Island, when his rowboat got away. The wind blew it across the pass to Insect Island, just around the corner from their floathouse. Knowing there was nothing he could do, he just kept on digging until the tide was too high. Leaving the sacks of clams safely anchored on the beach, he found a slab of wood and rolled it down to the water. Once afloat he knelt on the piece of driftwood and paddled with a stick across the dark pass toward the rowboat. He had just managed to reach the boat as Yvonne appeared around the corner, looking for him. She found her man wet and embarrassed, but safe.

Yvonne was getting used to the unexpected with Billy. The next worst thing after a runaway boat is one that won't run. Once Billy and his friend, Joe Caron, went duck hunting in Chop Bay, Knight Inlet, in a 16-foot scow with a seven hp West Bend outboard. As they neared their destination the motor quit. When they realized they were unable to fix it, they decided to start paddling for home. Though the southeast wind was with them, the tide was against and so they weren't making any headway. Then Billy noticed a four-by-eight sheet of plywood tacked down as a floor. They pulled up the floor and used it as a sail, reaching home in good time.

Life wasn't all digging clams and slinging fish. Billy loves working with wood and one winter he built a lovely little 13-foot skiff out of nailed and glued plywood. He smartened her up with a varnished mahogany bowcover and christened his handiwork *Gee Whiz*. In *Gee Whiz* Billy and Yvonne headed out in rain, snow, wind and darkness in search of a little diversion. A non-drinking man, Billy avoided the local moonshine operations. Instead, the couple would head for the Alert Bay theatre and bowling alley, often picking up a few friends from the mill at the Pearse Islands on their way.

Yvonne's sister Margaret left Vancouver as well, to marry Bud Brown, a local logger, and they tied their home in the tiny, south-facing bay on Davies Island. Bud and Margaret bought 16-mm films and invited everyone to the movies. Boats of all shapes and descriptions headed into their bay for the show. The films provided great entertainment for both adults and children, while the dogs tussled and sniffed outside. When the gathering came to an end, the guests called their dogs, climbed into their boats and disappeared into the night, whatever the weather. Some nights were beautifully calm, brilliant with moonlight; others were a thick, wet blackness or completely obscured by stinging snowflakes; regardless, the boats scattered into the night. Yvonne remembers crashing home in big westerly seas, a phosphorescent light show curling all around them.

Blacker than the night sky, the outline of the mountains guided Billy home at night, but logs were harder to see. One night travelling home alone, Billy hit an unlit log boom in the shadow of a hillside. When his boat jumped up onto the boom, Billy was knocked unconscious. As he came to, he was staring into the water, hanging by his belt from the bow cleat.

Racing about fullbore may seem reckless, but everyone felt much safer up the coast than in the cities. Surprisingly, very few accidents actually occurred and when they did, alcohol was usually a factor. People watched out for one another, providing a bit of a safety net. Twice a day, at 9:00 AM and 5:00 PM, the Coast Guard at Alert Bay radioed all the camps listed with them. If one didn't answer, a neighbour was sent to have a look. There was only one channel, #2292, and everyone listened in. Messages could be left

GEE WHIZ, *which Billy built one winter.* (PHOTO BY JAE PROCTOR)

COLUMBIA in Yokohama Bay, 1957. (PHOTO BY JAE PROCTOR)

with the Coast Guard for the camps and in this way news was relayed from the outside world.

The radio sets were large, unwieldy devices and a licence cost a whopping $100 a year. The antenna wire was exactly 206 feet long and was strung between two trees. The transmitters were built in Alert Bay, but to receive, a person had to have an AM radio as well. AM has a tremendous range, much farther than the VHF used by mariners today. Sitting in Greenway Sound, Billy was able to talk to boats nearly 150 miles away in Egmont.

The Columbia Coast Mission boat came around regularly and checked on everyone. If disaster fell, they were soon there to help out in any way they could. When Billy's father drowned, *Columbia* was in Seymour Inlet. They came as soon as they were notified, dropping anchor in Freshwater Bay three days later. Today's mission boats have kept up this tradition. Generous humanitarians (and great cooks), they are ready to help those in need regardless of religious beliefs or convictions.

Knowing how to be watchful without being intrusive is an art and Captain Ed Godfrey, skipper of *Columbia* from about 1930 to 1940, had it figured just right by all accounts. Jae was grateful for his regular visits. She suffered from pernicious anaemia, fainting often, and was treated with "liver shots" once every ten days. *Columbia* would approach remote floathouses slowly and idle along in front, giving people the chance to see him coming. Godfrey then leaned out of the wheelhouse to wave and have a few words with the families. If they looked like they needed company he stopped in; if not and it appeared that everyone was OK, the boat would move on. He was remembered with particular fondness.

"People just took to him," Yvonne recalled.

If a sick or injured person needed to get to the hospital in Alert Bay, *Columbia* often served as an ambulance. Familiar with navigating even the most difficult of channels by night and day, the experienced crew provided safe transport in all conditions. Time, of course, is crucial in saving lives and a boat as capable as *Columbia* was truly a godsend to people of the coast.

★★★

In 1960 Billy took a job falling snags for the Ministry of Forests in Tribune Channel, on Gilford Island across from Bond Sound. This time he was partnered with Lance Stephens. The two anchored their boats in the unprotected water in front of the claim, rowed ashore, and carried their chainsaws and tools three miles up a truck road just to get to the snags. One day, as they started cutting, a breeze began to blow from the southeast. They kept an eye on it and when they realized it was coming up fast they ran down to the beach. By the time they got there, it was blowing 40 knots, straight onto shore and they were relieved to see their boats were fine, although the rowboat had sunk. They bailed it out, climbed aboard and bucked the waves and wind out to the boats.

With the day still young, the two decided to run up into Bond Sound and go goose hunting. It wasn't safe to leave the boats where they were, so they anchored up near the flats in Bond and rowed ashore. The birds were plentiful and they knew their wives would be happy to cook up a delicious goose. They got a couple of geese and by the time they headed back to the boats, it was dark. When they looked out over the sound they realized they had forgotten to leave any lights on the boats. In the dark, they could just make out that their boats were not where they had left them. In fact, they were nowhere in sight.

It was still blowing a gale, but on this side of the channel, the wind was coming off the land, blowing their boats away. They set out in the rowboat and followed the wind along the shoreline. After searching for an hour they noticed a black shape out in the middle of the sound and decided it must be their boats. They started rowing toward them but the farther they got from shore, the bigger the waves became and they knew that if the dark shape was only a big root floating by and not their boats, it was going to be tough to get back to the beach. Much relieved, the men reached the boats, dragging anchor into deeper water. They were tired, and thankful to finally step aboard and fix a steaming cup of tea.

Another day, Billy was getting ready to fall a tree growing close to the beach. It was leaning out over the water and before he started cutting, he considered moving his rowboat. Instead, he decided this would be a test of skill. He would make that tree land exactly where he wanted it. Carefully he started making his cuts, but many factors dictate a tree's fall — the placement of branches, the slope, the wind and the shape of the trunk — and this tree didn't fall according to plan. It fell straight for the rowboat. Billy was sure the little boat was smashed, but found it instead neatly cut in half. That evening he perched gingerly on the stern half to row out to his big boat.

From the 1930s into the early '60s, the Department of Fisheries placed a bounty on all predators, to encourage people to exterminate them. They considered this an effective conservation measure for fish and deer. Fisheries even rigged a boat with a big knife on the bow, to cut in half every shark they encountered. Basking sharks fell prey easily to this vessel, as they lay on the surface. Unfortunately, their deaths did nothing to increase fish stocks because basking sharks eat plankton.

Billy was used to seeing one or two sharks every week in August and September, but soon the huge creatures disappeared, and they have never returned. Another Fisheries vessel, *Babine Post*, had a machine gun mounted on the bow to strafe seals and sea lions. Their intention was to reduce pressure on the rapidly dwindling salmon stocks. The bounty on predators was high and Fisheries required only some piece of the victim in exchange for a good reward:

Crow beak — 5¢
Raven beak — 50¢
Eagle beak — 50¢
Seal nose — $5
Wolf ear — $20
Cougar ear — $20

Despite the lack of any positive results from killing these species, the province of British Columbia is now seriously considering reinstating a seal kill, almost 40 years later. This time they are not acting out of ignorance. Fisheries' own studies show that only four percent of a seal's diet is salmon. Hake make up the bulk of their prey, 40%, and hake eat juvenile salmon. So killing seals will increase the salmon-consuming hake population and salmon will be harmed, not helped. The seals are a scapegoat to distract the public's attention away from the real problems: poor management, habitat destruction and too much human predation.

In the 1960s a living could be made hunting predators for these bounties. Billy remembers a boat pulling up at the Shell station in Alert Bay, its decks littered with crow corpses. One fisherman on *Sambo* earned his income in the off-season gillnetting harbour seals. He sold their pelts and collected the bounty. He had a heavy net constructed just for this purpose. Billy and Yvonne, ever in need of a little extra cash to get out from under the *Fisher Boy* debt, gave bounty hunting a try.

They set out on a winter day in *Gee Whiz* to shoot a seal. The inquisitive little marine mammals were plentiful and it wasn't long before one found them. Hunting seals is difficult because even though they are fat, they usually sink when they are shot, probably because they exhale as they submerge, dying, and so there isn't enough air in their lungs to float the corpse. The fledgling bounty-hunters managed to shoot the seal and then they raced to recover the body before it sank. Lunging simultaneously to grab it, they tipped the skiff and somehow fired the gun off across Yvonne's foot. Fortunately, her foot was all right, but *Gee Whiz* received a puncture wound. That was the end of seal hunting. It wasn't much to their taste to begin with and after that episode, they gave it up.

After only one fishing season, Billy sold *Fisher Boy*. He got a good price and bought a boat he really grew to love: *Dynamite II*. He finally had a truly good boat. A more reasonable 34 feet long, she was equipped with two nice bunks, a galley below decks and a pump sink. There wasn't a head, but since their house still did not have an indoor toilet either, it wasn't missed.

Yvonne appreciated a feature that lay beneath the waterline. Attached to the hull was a set of rolling chocks ten feet long and eight inches wide. These wooden runners prevented the boat from rolling very far to either side. As waves pushed against the boat, the chocks created resistance, absorbing the waves' energy, and returned the boat to an even keel before she had heeled over very far. With the stove from the old *Sea Gull* installed, this cosy new boat held the moist breath of the raincoast outside her door. Billy loved stepping into that wheelhouse.

Jae's fishbuying camp was tied to Billy and Yvonne's house and their collection of floats moved together down to Yokohama Bay each summer and then back inside the archipelago for the winter. In 1959, they wintered at Insect Island, the site of one of the largest ancient Native villages in the area. In 1960 and '61, they tied on the south side of Baker Island in a beautiful, calm, south-facing bay locally named Piling Bay.

While towing a floathouse is a relatively easy way of moving, it is not without its difficulties. When several floats are strung together there is considerably more drag than with just one float, so the boat doing the towing works harder. Not only is the weight greater with several floats, there is more resistance created by the wind and currents. Tugboats are very powerful, their innards dedicated almost entirely to horsepower. But the Proctors didn't own a tug, nor did they have the resources to charter one. To get the power they needed to tow the camp, they tied two fishboats together. One boat generally took the lead, steering the course, while the other provided additional pull. A boat moves forward by propelling water backward. Called "prop wash," this water pushes against anything in tow behind. Therefore, if the towline is too short, a boat pulls against its own push, slowing progress considerably. Increasing the distance between a boat and her tow allows the prop wash to dissipate, so when a floathouse is under tow, it rides far behind and out of earshot.

The seasonal Proctor migrations took a full day, so Yvonne stayed in her house as they headed south for another fishbuying summer and north for the winter. It was pleasant, watching the view change out the kitchen window. On land, each room in a house has characteristic light qualities, but in a moving floathouse the light changes. Dark rooms may get full sun, sunny rooms become shaded. The change is as refreshing as a new coat of paint. But when Yvonne glanced out the window on the 1960 tow south, she could see they were headed for disaster. The men steering the boats through Spring Pass were looking straight ahead, talking, and they didn't realize that while the boats were well clear of Green Rock, the houses were not. The floats had been caught by the tide

Floathouses anchored to the shore. (PHOTO BY ALEXANDRA MORTON)

and were swinging toward the rock. No amount of yelling was going to be heard by the skippers, so Yvonne watched helplessly as her house hit the rock.

The towline wrapped around Green Rock, pulling the boats hard over. This caused the men to jump up and look back. Float-logs were lunging to the surface like whales. Billy and Yvonne's float was old and waterlogged. To buoy it up, additional logs had been pulled underneath at right angles to the original float-logs. When these logs began to sink as well, another layer had been pulled under them. This process continued until there was an inverted pyramid of logs under their house. Instead of drawing two feet of water the float now drew closer to 15 feet. The logs at the very bottom hit the shallows of the reef first, and the momentum pushed them free. Luckily, no serious damage occurred, and the tow was soon underway again.

Later that year, a floathouse in tow from Shawl Bay to Malcolm Island was not so lucky. Crossing Queen Charlotte Strait in the pitch black of a stormy night, the boat arrived safely with only the float behind. The house had slid off the float and was drifting out to sea, only the roof visible.

In May of 1962, while towing south for Jae's last fishbuying season, the Proctors had their closest call. They left just before dawn, Yvonne, with her three-month-old daughter, Joanie, settled into Jae's house for the trip. Slowly the floats meandered through the narrow passes and protected water.

However, by mid-afternoon they were crossing the one small stretch at the west end of Midsummer Island that was wide open to Queen Charlotte Strait. Locally called the "Merry-Go-Round," because fishboats line up there one behind the other in a circle to catch coho, it is better known as a terrible place to be when the ebb tide meets the afternoon westerly. A hundred miles of Knight Inlet water is trying to get out, while the wind is pushing Queen Charlotte Strait back in. The resulting seas are steep and confused.

By the time the Proctor clan got to the Merry-Go-Round it was a roller coaster, with ten-foot waves. The two fishboats leaned into the tow and as they turned the corner the waves started to wash broadside to the floats. When waves hit the ends of logs they run

A floathouse under tow: TWILIGHT ROCK *tows Chris Bennett's Blackfish Lodge.*
(PHOTO BY ALEXANDRA MORTON)

harmlessly up in between them, but when they hit broadside, damage occurs. As the outside log rides up a wave, it strains against the cable lashing it to the next log. When that first log starts falling down the back of the wave, the second one is still riding up. This creates a rippling effect across the float, snapping all but the newest lashing. The steep waves rocked the house and Proctor dishes began clattering to the floor in both houses.

The women's concern over dishes turned to terror when the lashing holding their float together broke in several places. The logs fanned out and the entire house tilted as it began to slide into the water between the logs. Billy was constantly looking back at the houses and while "Grandma's" house was hidden behind his own, the angle of the roof told him all he needed to know. His mother, wife and daughter were in a house that was slipping into rough water.

He made the only move available to him; he turned to run with the waves into the protection of Owl Pass. Once the waves and float were moving in the same direction, there was far less stress on the lashing and the weight of the house held the float from fanning out completely. In the calm of Owl Pass Billy was able to get some ropes around the float and they were underway again. That fall, when it was time to move north Jae went to Vancouver and didn't return until her house was safely tied up for the winter.

How to Move a Big Rock and Use it as an Anchor
(essential information for the prospective floathouser)

You look along the beach at low tide and find a rock the right size. To make a good anchor, a rock should be about three tons, which is about three feet by four feet. You have to make sure it is loose and not stuck in the mud or sand. When you find one, drill two holes in it and put in a U-bolt. To make the bolt permanent take some sulphur powder and heat it up. It will melt. You pour that into the holes. Sulphur is one of the few things that expands when it cools and it will hold your bolt fast in the rock.

Well, now we have the rock and the U-bolt in it and we have to get it to the site. Tie a heavy anchorline to the rock. If you use a rope for this it is best to put a boomchain on the bolt first and

Securing two boomchains in a floathouse tie-up. (PHOTO BY ALEXANDRA MORTON)

tie the rope to the chain. This stops the rope from wearing on the rocks. Next, you will need a big log or a couple of smaller ones. Tie a short line to the U-bolt. It has to be strong enough to lift the rock, so use 1½ inch or bigger. When the tide comes in a bit, float the logs over the rock and tie the thick short rope around them as tight as you can. Now wait for the tide to rise higher and this will float the rock. As soon as it is free from the bottom you can tow it to the drop site.

Tie the free end of the anchorline to your float and then take the logs holding the rock out away from the float till the line comes tight. Hold it tight as you cut the rope around the logs with a sharp axe. As soon as that rock touches bottom you are anchored.

The best way to attach the anchorline to the float is to run it through a block hanging underneath the outer edge of the float and then tie it to a smaller rock, which will act as a counter weight. The block should be hung with a boomchain and the rock should be about 500 pounds, depending on what you are anchoring or how much tide and wind you have to contend with. You'll have to put a U-bolt in the smaller rock as well. Put the end of the anchorline through the block and tie it to the small rock, drop the big rock first, and then drop the small one. At low tide there should be about six feet of line between the rock being used as a counter weight and the block. The more scope you have on your anchorline, the less the counter weight will go up and down. Check and make sure the counter weight doesn't rest on the bottom during low tides.

I like this system of using a counter weight because it always holds everything tight and there is no slack anchorline at low tide. The more slack you have, the more you are going to move around in a blow and you could end up on the beach.

If a floathouse isn't tied up properly, it can look like this at low tide. (PHOTO BY ALEXANDRA MORTON)

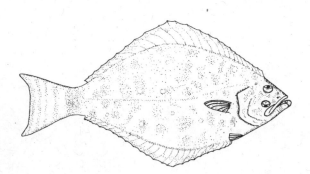

CHAPTER SIX

I sure did hate to see you go
But I guess we had to part.
I even shed a tear
And felt a sting in my heart.

Good-bye, Good luck
To the *Dynamite II.*

IN 1959 BILLY bought a boatshed and marine ways in Echo Bay, on Gilford Island, from Yvonne's cousin, Ralph Roth. Echo Bay is an ancient settlement, dating back 8,000 years. The pale cliffs above the bay still bear the red ochre paintings made by early human inhabitants. Their meaning has faded over time, but the pictographs resemble a sun and faces. The broad white clam-shell beach speaks of thousands of years of clam feasts. Rising up from this beach is a

106

high, flattened midden, the soil black with charcoal from prehistoric fires. The extent of it announces that grand Kwakiutl longhouses once stood there. It was an important village in the archipelago.

The north coast of British Columbia is one of the few places on this planet that has experienced steady human abandonment over the past hundred years. There were 10,000 Kwakiutl people living from Knight Inlet to Wells Pass, until they were horribly devastated by smallpox in the 1800s. All but three of their villages have been reclaimed by the rainforest. Gilford Village, Kingcome Village and Hope Town remain. Beginning in the late 1800s a few loggers, fishermen and homesteaders arrived with floathouses, and various canneries, salteries and shake mills sprang up, but they were short-lived and all have disappeared.

At the head of Kingcome Inlet, the Halliday family built a dike to dry out part of the Kingcome River flood plain. They built a large home and a barn complete with concrete floors. The Hallidays rowed to Campbell River every year and every second year they say Mrs. Halliday went along to have a baby. However, the rainforest is repossessing their homestead now too.

The Halliday home in Kingcome Inlet. (PHOTO BY ALEXANDRA MORTON)

Every bay offering any degree of protection shows evidence of human occupation, but a person has to know where to look, as the signs are fading rapidly. Echo Bay is known as the "place of gathering power" by its Kwakiutl inhabitants. It is one of the last bays in the area still embracing humanity within its curves.

Gilford Island is separated from the mainland by Tribune Channel. At 150 square miles, Gilford is one of the largest islands on the coast of British Columbia. Its highest point is Mount Reid, 5,200 feet above sea level. The area from Drury Inlet to Johnstone Strait is called the Broughton Archipelago by government agencies, but the residents of the area simply call it the Mainland.

In the fall of 1857 a high-ranking Bella Coola man and his wife went fishing in Bond Sound, Tribune Channel. Several families from Gilford Village were there and a woman from Gilford reportedly stole a very valuable Hamatsa whistle belonging to the Bella Coola man. Stealing was a capital offence. The next fall the Bella Coola attacked Gilford Village in revenge. Half the warriors went to the east end of the village and half to the west. When it was almost daylight they attacked and killed all but seven men

Old fore-and-aft road, Claydon Bay. (PHOTO BY ALEXANDRA MORTON)

The shingle-bolt mill in Echo Bay, 1922. (COLLECTION OF YVONNE SCOTT)

and five women. Gilford was abandoned for many years after the raid, until some people moved down from a big village in Wakeman Sound.

Europeans came to Gilford Island in 1880, among them the first handloggers. They came in rowboats and their shacks sprang up around the island. Soon after loggers using horses and oxen arrived, a shingle-bolt mill was established in Echo Bay and horse camps appeared in Tribune Channel, Knight Inlet and Port Elizabeth. In 1897 the Powell River Company started logging Gilford Island with a steam donkey. They built "fore-and-aft" roads, some over a mile long. A fore-and-aft road was essentially a chute constructed with three logs. Fallen trees were rolled onto these "roads" and dragged down to the water; the longest log road on Gilford was in Shoal Harbour.

As more loggers came into the area, they brought new techniques to get logs to saltwater. Lakes were dammed and water levels raised to float logs from one lake to the next. They built big wooden troughs called "flumes." When a lake was filled with logs the loggers opened the gates of the dam and floated the logs down the flume to the sea. This is the way Scott Cove was logged in 1918. While it worked well for the loggers, salmon were unable to reach their spawning grounds because of the dams and the diversion of water to the flumes.

Loggers also built chutes on hillsides to slide logs down to the sea. Then came the A-frame loggers and skyline loggers. A-frames are two logs lashed together at one end, set upright in the shape of an "A," and held rigid with guylines. A cable passes through a block at the peak of the "A." The skyline was a heavy cable strung between two A-frames. With a powerful winch, logs could be moved a considerable distance suspended on the cable. In 1927 a railroad logger came to Viner Sound, built a railroad and logged there for eight years. A railroad was also built in Retreat Pass at about the same time.

A-frame logging lasted over 50 years, but other techniques came as well. Some loggers used Caterpillar tractors to move their wood and some used skidders. Most went broke. The first truck logging was in Scott Cove in 1939 on a plank road. A sawmill started up around 1948 in Gilford Bay, Knight Inlet, to cut railroad ties for export to Pakistan. Logging was a diverse industry, owned and operated by many families, not the handful of huge companies as it

An A-frame under tow. (PHOTO BY ALEXANDRA MORTON)

is today. Those families lived on or near their claims and created communities with stores, post offices, schools and freight boats. The majority of money earned was spent locally.

Today, there are only two international logging corporations on Gilford — Interfor and MacMillan Bloedel — with miles and miles of roads. Their main log dumps are in Scott Cove, Shoal Harbour and Gilford Bay. The men who work here don't own the company, don't live here, and never bring their families. They are called in and laid off at the whim of company owners who have never been to Gilford Island. The money is dispersed south, mostly to shareholders who have never seen Gilford Island and have no idea of the impact of their company.

The first post office in the area was established in 1904 and run by a man named Emerson, in Emerson Bay, Greenway Sound. By 1908, handloggers were working in Tribune Channel, so he moved his store and post office closer to them, into Simoom Sound. About this time John Dunseith, who was married to one of Emerson's daughters, took over the post office. In 1936, a post office was approved for the store in Echo Bay. This would have been a major competitor for Dunseith so to prevent it, Dunseith moved his post office down to a bay soon nicknamed "Little Simoom," right beside Echo Bay. Echo Bay was not allowed to start up its own post office with Dunseith so close. In 1973 Ray Rossback bought the post office and moved it into Echo Bay. Today, the sign on the post office in Echo Bay still reads "Simoom Sound."

When the store was in "Little Simoom" almost everyone did their shopping there. Families had a standing order for vegetables and milk. When the freight boat arrived once a week you had to take what you ordered, no matter if you wanted it or not. The mail came on the boat as well. When I was away Yvonne would row over to the store.

A hotel and pub were built in Echo Bay in 1933. A school opened in the 1920s and was provided with a new building in 1960. Miraculously, it is still open. From 1950 to 1968 a Forestry station operated at Echo Bay.

There are 15 lakes on the island, (86 if you count the pot holes), and eight streams that bear salmon today: Viner Creek, Scott Cove creek, Shoal Harbour creek, Maple Bay creek, Health Lagoon, Wahkana Bay creek, Duck Creek and Gilford Creek. Cutthroat trout, Dolly Varden, steelhead, chum, coho, a few pinks and the odd sockeye all use these creeks Most of the salmon streams have been damaged by one or more logging practices, but they are being repaired by the community living here today. Half a million salmon once spawned on Gilford Island, but now there are only about 40,000 in a good year. In addition, Gilford provides habitat for four wolf packs, many black bears, mink, raccoons, deer, otter, weasel, beaver, red squirrel, flying squirrel, mice, voles, moles, bats, shrews, snakes, toads, frogs and salamanders.

★★★

The boat ways Billy bought sat on the white shell beach of Echo Bay. Close scrutiny of the beach reveals a truly wondrous array of human handiwork from stone and bone tools to square-sided boat nails. Two distinct human eras are reshuffled daily by the rise and fall of the tides.

Experience had taught Billy that the best way to survive was to become as diverse as possible. Between fishing, clam digging, logging, trapping and the boat ways, he supported his family without having to work for a company. The ways never contributed a big income, but like everything else, it helped, and he enjoyed it. He charged ten dollars to haul a boat out of the water and it could stay there for up to a month and return to the water on the same bill. If it stayed longer than a month he charged a dollar a day, but this was enforced only once. During the life of the ways Billy pulled up 736 boats total, 35 a year.

At first, Billy did all the repair work and bottom painting himself, but when he developed a strong allergic reaction to the anti-fouling, red lead paint, he changed his policy and let the skippers do their own work. Proctor's boatshed was located at the heart of the community, near the school, community hall, post office, Forestry office and bar, so it became a gathering place. There was a constant knot of people standing around talking with whoever was working on his boat. There was something very enjoyable about spending time at Billy's ways. People shared stories and talked, watching the boat owner at work. In remote places, good conversation is very highly prized.

When dances were held, Billy found cases of beer stashed in his lumber pile. For some, it didn't feel like a party without a couple of drinks between dances and they knew their alcohol was safe with Proctor.

The boatshed was next to the schoolyard and the children liked to visit too. Some were not entirely welcome company. One afternoon, young Bobby Brash took aim with a clod of dirt and hit Billy on his head as he worked beneath *Dynamite II*. There was no reaction so next the boy threw a stick. Still nothing. Feeling really bold, Brash dropped an egg-sized rock on Billy's head. More tolerant than most, Billy ignored the assault until the rock hit him and then he lit. Streaking out from under the boat he caught the boy and sent him home bawling.

Years later, the two met again when a helicopter alighted at the Proctors' homestead and out stepped a man with a familiar face.

Twilight Rock up in the boatshed. (Photo by Alexandra Morton)

"Remember me?" Billy remembered all right. Brash was now working for Forestry and had been sent to see if Billy's sawmill was cutting wood legally. Billy bought a small mill in 1987 and with his log salvage licence collected logs escaped from booms or from slides. Even a log that has been lying on a beach for ten years must be scaled and money paid to the provincial government before it can be used. Brash was making sure Proctor was doing this. The mill checked out OK, but Billy was left wondering at the sense of humour that rules the universe.

Billy had a policy of not pulling up the boats of people he didn't know, particularly tourists. He had no liability insurance and didn't want to get into a legal tangle with a complete stranger if a boat got damaged.

One yachtsman refused to take no for an answer. As Billy explained his policy the tourist kept insisting, "I'm a little different."

Head down, hands deep in his pockets, Billy steadfastly repeated, "Nope, no way. I don't cater to tourists."

Billy was scheduled to pull a friend's boat up in 12 hours, but he eventually gave in and slid the 28-foot *Puppet* up for just one tide,

Running the sawmill. (PHOTO BY ALEXANDRA MORTON)

Neighbours coming to Proctors' at high tide to pick up their lumber orders. (PHOTO BY ALEXANDRA MORTON)

certain it would do the tourist no good. *Puppet* had suffered a run-in with a bit of B.C.; both shafts were bent and the propellers damaged.

Once *Puppet* was up, Billy headed home for lunch. When he returned, he was amazed to see what the unassuming man had accomplished in less than an hour. He'd pulled both shafts and replaced them (he carried six spares), the propellers and the key. Billy was impressed. He thought all tourists were completely unfamiliar with the undersides of their own boats. His "rule," however, went back into effect the moment the cruiser re-entered the water.

When Echo Bay became a provincial park, Billy was told his boatshed had to go, so in 1988 he built another one on his own property. He constructed the enormous platform and then, using a chainsaw winch, pulled the massive laminated arches up one by one. When he pulled up the last arch, the shed looked like a gigantic whale skeleton. For an instant the arches lined up as evenly as ribs but then the last arch kept on moving, crashing into its neighbour, which bent and hit the next one and so on. It looked, for one awfully long moment, as if the entire shed was going to

The last arch going up on the new boatshed. (PHOTO BY ALEXANDRA MORTON)

collapse, but it stopped halfway along. The spectators tensed, expecting bellows of rage. Instead, Billy's distinctive chuckle built into a belly-laugh.

"Christ!" he said. "You can't let a little thing like that get to you!"

***

At one time the Nimpkish River was the biggest salmon-producing river between the Fraser River and Cape Caution. Before the 1920s the Nimpkish had more than a million sockeye and runs of 300,000 chinooks. Then the drag seine came and B.C. Packers built a cannery in Alert Bay to process the Nimpkish fish. B.C. Packers had over 20 drag seines in the river, but still, there were good runs until 1957.

In 1957, the B.C. Forest Service did an aerial spray of the north end of Vancouver Island. They sprayed from Blinkhorn Peninsula in Johnstone Strait to Cape Scott, Nigei Island and Hope Island. They sprayed with DDT and they did it in May, just when all the fry and smolts were leaving the rivers.

116

The reason they sprayed was to kill a bug that was killing spruce trees. I was in Goletas Channel on my way home from Bull Harbour when they were spraying Nigei Island. They used two big four-engine planes and they had a thousand gallons of DDT in each plane. There were holes along each wing and as they went there was a fog behind them. This went on for a week or more.

There were stories of people with wheelbarrows full of dead tiny fry from the banks of the Nimpkish River. After that, there were no big runs of coho or springs to the Nimpkish River.

In 1962, many of B.C.'s commercial salmon fishermen figured their way of life had ground to a halt.

The salmon stocks took a severe drop in the early 1960s, mainly for two reasons. The herring fleet with their high-powered Mercury lights attracted all the fish. They caught a lot of baby salmon. I went along on a seiner in Knight Inlet and he gave me a bucket of herring. There were 47 herring and seven small springs in just that one dip into the hatch.

Then around 1964, B.C. Packers started summer herring fishing. Before that it was a winter fishery. Herring seines were real deep. In September of 1964 the B.C. Packers fleet came into Fife Sound. The odd boat would let the salmon go, but a lot of them just brailed them aboard and headed for Namu. They wiped out the chums in a lot of places.

When they used Mercury lights everyone called them the "grilse fishermen" because they caught so many baby salmon, known as grilse.

Suddenly, there were no fish. In 1962, Billy had the dubious honour of being "high boat," by earning a mere $1,500, which was not enough to support his family. In response to the low numbers of returning salmon, Fisheries closed many areas. It didn't look good. Traditional fishing grounds were barren and who was to blame? Loggers were damming streams, preventing salmon from going upriver, and clear-cut logging was killing eggs on the spawning beds. Salmon eggs incubating in gravel need a constant flow of water to survive, and when a hillside is clear-cut, the soil washes downhill with each rainfall, clogging the little spaces between the pebbles and smothering the eggs. Clear-cutting also warms river water, which is deadly to the cool-loving salmon.

Pesticides were flowing into the creeks, poisoning juvenile fish. Relentless, increasing fishing pressure meant fewer and fewer salmon were returning to these damaged rivers, further decreasing survival. No one knew what was happening to the fish once they were out to sea. Warm currents, lack of food and increased predation kill salmon where we never see it.

In addition, the salmon runs of each stock fluctuate. Some years the runs are naturally small and at times, the smallest cycles of several runs all coincide in one year. Some salmon mature and return in two years, others four, five, six and possibly seven. Therefore, any given year will have a different combination of runs of each species. Generally, there are a few good runs and a few small ones. Sometimes several big runs of sockeye, coho and springs will coincide for a bumper year or, as in 1962, all the small runs come in together.

This is how to predict the timing of the salmon runs in Area 12 [from Kelsey Bay to Bright Island, just east of Pine Island]. It is all to do with the full moon. If the first full moon of the year is late, the salmon runs will be late. If the first full moon is early, the runs will be early. Some years the first full moon is around January 3 or 4 and some years it is around January 24. The spring salmon show in the inlets on the fifth full moon of the year, May 3 to May 25. All salmon make major moves on the full moon tides and just minor moves on new moon tides. The pinks that spawn in the Mainland inlets show up on the sixth full moon of the year. Fraser River sockeye and pinks that go through Blackfish Sound always show on the full moon tides, the early runs are there on the seventh moon. The late runs of Fraser sockeye and pinks show on the eighth moon. This is based on 50 years of waiting, watching and fishing.

But even a poor year should have been better than 1962. Jae quit buying fish for good at the end of that season. To avoid another lean winter, Billy took *Dynamite II* beachcombing, looking for saleable logs that had escaped from various booms or been carried to sea by a landslide. Billy really enjoyed beachcombing, cruising in and out of every bay, but it didn't quite make ends meet. So, in 1963 Billy and Mel Bellveal became partners and headed back to the sidehills to do a little handlogging for themselves.

The concept of getting a tree into the water without winches, an A-frame, trucks or even a horse is difficult to grasp. Trees are immensely heavy plants, as anyone who has wrestled with firewood can appreciate. To move a log into the water, the type and size of tree, its placement and the hillside itself all have to be just right. A handlogger's primary tools were a chainsaw, wedges, Gilchrist jacks and, Billy claims, "a strong back and a weak mind!" The number one difficulty was a cursed event known as a "hangup."

At the time Billy handlogged, it was an easy business to get into. He just cruised the coastline until he found an area he could work; then he applied for the timber sale, put down a $60 deposit and was up the hill cutting ten days later. The sales were one mile long and ten "chains" deep. A chain is 66 feet and was measured straight back into the hillside at sea level, so when the sale (or claim) was steep, it often covered an actual 1,800 feet of slope. If the amount of wood cut and sold equalled what Forestry estimated was there, they sent back the deposit, thus ensuring that the claims were logged. Each logger was allowed only two timber sales at any one time; the government tried to disperse this resource to as many people as possible.

Handlogging is not easy. Only trees on a specific kind of terrain — trees on a steep hillside that dropped straight down into the ocean — could be harvested and they had to be handled carefully. Billy and Mel's first task was to haul their very heavy tools up the hill, including a chainsaw and two Gilchrist jacks weighing 60 pounds apiece. Just downhill from the target tree, Billy would cut two alders or other unsaleable trees across the hill, parallel to each other and the beach. Then he started cutting the tree he wanted. As

119

soon as his saw was completely embedded in the trunk, he placed wedges in behind it. By tapping the wedges carefully with the back of the axe, he directed where the tree would fall. If a tree dropped in the wrong place, he had to leave it behind, so this was a crucial stage of the operation.

When the tree was down, its top pointing toward the sea, Billy trimmed off the branches, cut off the top and peeled a six-inch strip of bark away from the entire length of the log to make it slippery. The peeling was done with glancing blows of a small axe. Next, the two jacks were used to roll the log onto the smooth, peeled strip. As he pumped the jacks, the log rolled over inch by inch, until it began to slide. Billy loved standing inches away as a massive log thundered past him to the sea.

Ideally, the log crashed unchecked into the inlet within seconds of take-off, but often a day or more was required to get a log wet. If it hit a stump or a boulder, that was a hangup, and was probably responsible for more foul language in the woods than any other one event. Slipping and sliding down to wherever the log was hung up, Billy had to assess the situation.

What made the difference between profit and wasted effort was knowing how a log would respond to a little push here or there from the jacks. Where was the weight of it resting and at what point would the log roll or just pivot? The wrong shove might wedge it into a spot where he couldn't move it again and would have to abandon it.

While difficult, this type of logging worked financially because the tools were so inexpensive. Billy didn't need to invest a huge sum of money in equipment, so he didn't have to fall a great number of trees to make a profit. Some handloggers made the mistake of buying bigger and bigger winches. It was tempting, after having to leave valuable logs behind due to bad hangups. But the winches required a crew and more trees, and a vicious circle was begun. A team of handloggers could do well for themselves if they resisted the call for more power. Billy really enjoyed the challenges of handlogging, even if it wasn't as profitable as fishing. A big tree high on a hillside still catches his eye with its silent dare. Could he put that one in?

After 1963 I was away from home a lot so Yvonne had the kids most of the time by herself. I would start fishing in April and go till September 20th. Then I went handlogging, but I would be home every night. Then I would trap for six weeks and be away most of the time. I was away too much; the kids made strange when I got home.

When I was handlogging I towed the trees home each night. When I had 70 or so I bucked them up into logs, and Yvonne would shove them through a gap into a bag boom. She liked that job and she took it seriously. She kept the logs all lined up, never let one go crosswise. Sometimes guys visiting would see her working and take her pike pole. She was reluctant to give it up, because it made her mad as hell if they shoved the logs through any old way.

When they were out looking for a new claim, Billy and Mel saw a stretch of shoreline in Tribune Channel that looked really good. The slope was steep and there were lots of big trees on it. They couldn't figure out why no one had logged it yet so they applied for the lease and were soon hauling the heavy Gilchrist jacks up the mountainside. The first tree was a beauty. It slid down the hill exactly as planned, slowed for a tense couple of seconds, then dove into the ocean and — disappeared.

All Mel and Billy could do when they got to the beach was scratch their heads. There was no sign of their beautiful log — it must have stuck in the sea floor. When a tree slides down a 1,200-foot slope, it can dive down 200 to 300 feet and take five minutes to float back up to the surface. However, the shores of Tribune Channel were perfect for handlogging because they went straight down over 400 feet. A soft bottom holds a log the way a round of wood holds a thrown knife, but Tribune wasn't soft. The next log did exactly the same thing, so Billy and Mel decided to quit for the day and puzzle this out for a bit.

The next morning Billy returned at low tide in *Dynamite II*. He slowly cruised the area where the logs had disappeared and found the fresh-cut butt of one of their logs gleaming, a pale circle 40 feet down. The log was sticking straight up, but what was holding it?

With great difficulty he sank a noose around it and tied the line to his boat. He had to pull hard in all directions to loosen the log but finally it rose. Clam shell was clinging to the bark for the first 16 feet of the log; it had been driven that far into the sand.

Billy crisscrossed the area with his sounder and saw the problem. While the bottom dropped straight away from the shore for the first 80 feet, it rose back up and then plunged down again. This dip had filled with clam shell and formed a log trap. After a bit of experimenting, Billy and Mel discovered that if they could get a log going fast enough, it would jump the shelf into deep water. A big red cod floated to the surface after one log disappeared, apparently hit or stunned by the diving log. The fish was promptly scooped up and made a fine dinner.

In addition to rolling logs into the water with jacks, Billy pulled logs in with his boat. This could be very hard on the boat and he learned to run an extremely long piece of line to the log. When a big log hit the water it was going to go down a long way and if it ran out of line, it would try to take his boat down with it. Though he took care to do the job right, funny things had a way of happening. Once, in preparation for pulling a particular hundred-foot balsam off a steep slope, Billy let out 400 feet of towline and gave the boat a good snort ahead. When the line pulled taut, the log started to come fast. However, as it neared the beach it veered and passed behind a big cedar. Billy was going ahead at six knots until the line snugged up to the cedar and suddenly he was going backwards straight for the beach, still at six knots. Fortunately, the log came to a stop and he was able to hold his boat off the beach.

After Billy put a log in the water he brought his boat alongside, tied to the log and hopped off to trim away the branches. Once, while he was trimming a low-floating hemlock, his knot slipped and he drifted a hundred feet away, to the end of the towline. This was normally not a problem; he could just pull himself in with the towline (which had been used to bring the log down the hill). But this time, the weight of the cable between the log and the rope had pulled the end of the hemlock under water. Billy sat down on the log and inched his way toward the cable.

As he slid forward the log sank. By the time he got to where the cable was, he was in water up to his armpits. The heavy, ten-foot choker, made of ⅝-inch cable, hung straight down into the cold sea. It was a tricky balancing act, trying to swing the cable up with his feet to his hands without leaning over too far and falling off the log, and all the more dangerous because Billy still couldn't swim.

Billy's little *Dynamite II* took a beating logging. Once, the top of a big tree broke off with 300 feet of towline out and came sailing right over the crosspiece on the mast, tearing all the antennas off.

The old *Dynamite* was a double-ender with a sternpost that stuck up. I was always going to cut it off level with a chainsaw because it got in the way. I had a big yellow cedar timber across the deck, attached with a cable around the bow. When I was pulling a log, that cable slipped off one end of the timber. It flew around and hit the sternpost and took that sternpost right out of the boat! I idled into Echo Bay, dropped the cradle, and drove the boat onto it. I put the come-along on the sternpost, pulled all the nails out and kind of trimmed the ends off the planking. Then I put a couple of bolts across with boards along the outside to pull it back together. I spiked it and I was back handlogging that afternoon. That happened three different times. Finally, I had to put in a big wide sternpost. Everybody said if I kept the boat any longer she was going to have a square stern.

One time I went to Telegraph Cove and bought a six-by-six piece of edge-grain yellow cedar. Oh, it was a beautiful piece of wood. It was stupid to make a mast out of it. Anyway, I sanded it all up, oiled it, put it up and tried pulling a log off a tall bluff, just using my mast. I needed a couple of boomsticks and I had just gotten that sale. I told Yvonne, "I'm not going to bother putting the timber on, I'll just go down and pull from the mast."

Well, I didn't put two wraps around the mast. I just went around the mast and tied a bowline. When I went ahead on it the line slid up the mast and broke it in three pieces. The bottom third of the mast hooked the hatch cover and it flew back and bent the rudderstock. Oh God, I think I tore three masts out of the *Dynamite*.

The boat wasn't the only one getting hurt. When the dog (a piece of metal which holds the gear on the jack in position) broke on his haywire old Gilchrist jack, the handle slammed up, hitting Billy behind the ear. It moved so fast he didn't know what was going on. When he came to, he was on his hands and knees about five feet from the jack, and there was a roaring in his ears as he crawled over to it. Trying to figure out what had happened, he found a roll of skin from his neck stuck to the handle. That made things clear.

On another fine day, Billy was up on Owl Island falling for Hank Roth with a brand new, ten hp Titan chainsaw. The saw was cutting fine until he started to fall a mature hemlock. A strong gust of wind hit, pushing the tree over sideways, and as it fell the saw went with it. The tree landed with its butt end 20 feet up in the air and when the top flopped to the ground, the saw was flung free. It sailed through the air, hit the stump and broke in two. Then the tree slid downhill, over the saw, and when it rolled off, the saw was on fire. That evening all Billy had to take home was the saw's bar, and it was bent.

Once enough logs were in the water, Billy called his broker, who arranged for a tug, and the wood was towed south to Howe Sound where it was scaled. Billy paid for the tow, but his wood was insured as soon as the tug hooked on to it.

Handlogging was relatively easy on the forest because no roads were cut or sorting areas flattened, and the small cuts regenerated quickly. Also, no one could log far from the ocean and the gentle slopes of the estuaries were untouched. But in the early 1970s handlogging was made more difficult when government policies shifted, favouring corporate logging.

Handlogging was good until around 1975 when the beachcombers down in the gulf and Howe Sound went dry. All the loggers started to bundle their logs with cables and no more logs escaped out of the booms, so there were none to pick up any more. A lot of those beachcombers moved up here to the Mainland. Suddenly in 1976, there were 127 handlogging sales applied for in this area. There was so much demand that the Forest Service put the timber sales up for auction. Anyone could bid for them. In 1968 all handloggers had been put on a quota system. They took an average of what you had put in the water for three years previously and that was your quota for the year. I had a good quota. I was allowed 300,000 feet because I'd been logging every winter. But a lot of guys ended up with a small quota. If you held a sale you never worked in those three years, you only got 60,000 board feet. In 1976 they took the quota system off when they started public auctions.

The last sale I had was in 1979. There got to be so many rules and red tape that I just gave up.

★★★

The Story of an Old Cedar Tree

This is the story of one of the oldest cedar trees in the Broughton Archipelago. It is growing on the peninsula formed by Watson Cove in Tribune Channel.

1700 BC — The cedar is just starting to grow. This is the birth of the Olmec civilization on the southern coast of the Gulf of Mexico.

1400 BC — The cedar is 300 years old and about 70 feet tall. It suffered some hardship and is split 20 feet above the ground and has two tops. It has also lost some bark. The firs around it are taller, but many are dying and falling down. This is the time of the end of the Minoan civilization.

1200 BC — The cedar is 500 years old and has four tops; it is 80 feet tall and 30 inches in diameter. Hemlock and balsam are growing fast and straight beside the cedar, which at 500, is still young for its species.

700 BC — The cedar is 1000 years old. The surrounding trees have taken up much of the nutrients and the cedar is growing very slowly. One top was hit by lightning but luckily the fire didn't burn the rest of the tree. At a thousand years old the tree is big enough now to support an eagle's nest. A few people came and made a summer camp. They caught fish and hung them to dry, but decided it was a poor place for a permanent camp and moved on.

Cedar seedling. (DRAWING BY ALEXANDRA MORTON)

400 BC — The cedar is 1300 years old. A big snowfall broke a limb and left a big scar. That winter the goats and deer moved down to sea level. The people found hunting good near the cedar and they found the cedars nearby tall and straight for canoes and longhouse posts. They grew straight because there is a big bluff to the south and the resulting shade makes the trees grow fast and straight to reach the sunlight. The big cedar is starting a burl ten feet above the ground. Alexander the Great conquers Egypt.

100 BC — At 1600 years the cedar is over 100 feet tall and eight feet in diameter. The people come every winter to hunt and eat many clams, leaving the shells lying around the base of the tree. The Silk Road opens between China and the western world.

300 AD — The cedar is 2000 years old. There is a community around the base with two longhouses and two more across the

bay under the bluffs. A landslide created a beautiful waterfall that shimmers with rainbows in the sun. The Huns invade northern China, breaking up the Chinese empire.

800 AD — The cedar is 2500 years old. Three hundred years ago a huge storm blew down many surrounding trees, and in their rotting fibre the big cedar reseeded future generations which now surround their parent. The people built another longhouse and the community has thrived on all the game and on the salmon, which school in the bay in dry years. They laid hemlock branches on the beach for the herring to spawn on, then hung the branches to dry and ate the rich roe. A rock slide buried the two longhouses across the bay, when the people were away fishing. When they returned much of their village was gone and they had to establish a new site before winter. Charlemagne is crowned Emperor of the Holy Roman Empire.

1500 AD — At 3200 years old the cedar has stopped getting any taller as the tops are dead. Its heart has started to rot, rain somehow finding its way in. Owls have nested in the tree for years, mink have dens in the roots and the mountain goats know to visit the lowlands around the tree during the harshest winters. Europeans "discovered" the continent in 1492.

1800 AD — The cedar is 3500 years old and 13 feet in diameter. The tree has outlived its neighbours because it never grew very tall. This saved it from the strongest winds and from becoming a canoe or a longhouse post. Six years ago Captain Vancouver sailed right by the big cedar to anchor at Deep Sea Bluff.

1994 AD — In the last hundred years handloggers passed the old tree. The ground was too flat for them to log near the tree, but they lived in the bay and stored their logs there. Right after the First World War more loggers came. They had a steam donkey and built a fore-and-aft road close to the cedar. An A-frame logger fell the trees all around the cedar and so it swayed in the wind. However, the blowdown hundreds of years earlier had created strong roots in the tree and it held. A salmon farm moved in nearby and they tied their mort grinder below the big tree. The tubs of chemicals and rotting fish kept most other boaters away. There are fewer salmon and almost no herring, but at 15 feet across the old cedar still stands. Thousands of eagles have taken their first flight from the branches of the old cedar.

The cedar tree in Billy's story. (PHOTO BY ALEXANDRA MORTON)

CHAPTER SEVEN

Have you watched the birds fly back and forth
Or heard the honk of a goose as he goes north
Without longing to go somewhere too
Where you could always do as you wanted to?

IN 1972 BILLY decided it was time for a new boat. He had the money, and it was his dream to have a truly *new* boat, built to his own specifications. In September he phoned Chris Frostad and a few weeks later he was on his way to Vancouver to pick out the design. It had been 21 years since he had gone to Vancouver.

Billy gave Frostad a $3,000 deposit. When the hull had ribs and was ready to be planked, Billy sent another $7,000, and when the engine went in, $10,000. As the boat approached completion Billy went back to Vancouver, but endless delays stretched out to a month and he returned home. Finally, she was launched and Billy could bring her home. He owed another $1,500, but Frostad trusted him to pay at the end of the fishing season and he let the boat go, wishing Billy good luck.

When Billy got home there was a cheque for $10,000 waiting for him from his last boom of logs, so he owned the spunky little troller free and clear. Two days later he pulled her up on his ways in Echo Bay. Yvonne broke a bottle of champagne on her bow and christened her *Twilight Rock,* a place close to where Billy and Yvonne had met.

In the 1960s and '70s, hard work made for a good life, while today, hard-working couples often find themselves deeply in debt for the simple pleasure of owning their own homes. As the debts grow, they both have to work full time and are unable to raise their children themselves.

Twilight Rock was designed to fish the inside waters east of Vancouver Island, but the Department of Fisheries and Oceans began closing more and more areas in an effort to bring the fish back. Instead of fully examining what was happening up the rivers on the spawning beds, the government chose simply to close fishing grounds; it was easier. Fishermen are more controllable than the powerful logging companies cutting timber deep in the watershed valleys.

Logging practices and the lack of trees on hillsides caused changes so profound that fish were increasingly unable to reproduce. Mature trees growing on a slope regulate the flow of rainwater draining into the rivers. The forest canopy cools the runoff water; the tree roots filter it and absorb billions of gallons. When trees are removed from a large area, the rainwater races downhill unchecked, picking up soil as it goes. Without the dark green canopy, the exposed ground bakes in the sun, heating the water which passes over it. High water temperatures weaken or stress fish, making them less able to feed, more vulnerable to attack by predators and more susceptible to diseases and parasites.

Too much soil in a river packs the gravel with mud. Ideally, salmon eggs incubate in the spaces within pebbly gravel. Each species needs a different size of stone. The water running through the gravel washes and supplies oxygen to the eggs. When mud paves the gravel, freshly laid eggs have no nooks and crannies to lie in, and wash downstream to their death.

With the closures, Billy had no choice but to head back out to the west coast. At 37 feet, *Twilight Rock* was five feet shorter than *Fisher Boy*, and would bob even more in the ocean swells. Still, Billy realized he had to try fishing the open water again. This time it wasn't an adventure; it was the only way he was going to keep on fishing, and he was determined to make a go of it.

By the 1970s, most of the fishbuying companies had folded because there weren't enough fish being caught in the Blackfish Sound area, so Billy started selling his fish to Seafoods Products in Port Hardy. Seafoods was a good company and Billy has stuck with them from the start. In 1974, he went to Seafoods, loaded up with ice and food, and then, with seasickness pills on the window sill, headed out Goletas Channel to the Pacific Ocean.

Twilight Rock is a sprightly little boat and she squeaked happily to the rhythm of the swell as her wooden ribs were squeezed and twisted by the waves. Her poor skipper was not nearly so cheerful

Talking on the radio aboard TWILIGHT ROCK. (PHOTO BY ALEXANDRA MORTON)

and spent much of his time on his knees, gripping the guylines with his head over the side. Slowly, Billy's gut hardened because it was a case of fish out here or don't fish at all. If he took an inside licence he would have been banished to the Gulf of Georgia where the fish were getting scarcer all the time. So, sick as he was, Billy began learning how to fish the vast west coast.

Billy's older daughter, Joanie, worked as his deckhand for several years to earn money for school. Unlike her father, Joanie loved school and she didn't get seasick. She brought her guinea pig, Guineas, along. Guineas was a good little sea-going pig and would sit beside Billy looking out the window, chattering away. If Guineas got left out on the hatch when rain started to fall, his high-pitched squeals brought a prompt rescue. He often had the run of the boat and his only fault was the occasional little "beans" he left behind.

At age 17, Joanie was tough. Once, when Billy got very sick from a combination of seasickness and the anti-seasick medication, Joanie had to bring the boat over "the bar" alone into the safe anchorage of Bull Harbour where her dad could recover.

At first, Billy ventured just beyond Goletas Channel to fish the Vancouver Island shoreline. While there weren't a lot of fish, most of them were springs and Billy could anchor safely near shore, escaping the sickening swell for a couple of hours. Next he went out to the "Yankee Bank" where *Twilight Rock* became a fixture. This bank is a broad, submerged plain where a boat is constantly lurching about in the huge "lump," as the fishermen call the swell, produced by shallow water. The shallow water, however, is part of what makes the Yankee Bank productive. Billy watched carefully where the other boats fished and paid close attention to his sounder. Soon that piece of ocean became familiar to him. He found "The Gully" and fished it hard. Despite a huge increase in his fuel bill, Billy was surviving at fishing again.

In addition to the lump, the frightening thing about the Yankee Bank is how far it is from safe anchorage. It takes about an hour and a half to get to the protection of Vancouver Island and in the summer westerlies, the trip gets pretty rough. As the ocean bottom shallows, the waves grow and shorten, and after a while it feels as though the boat is going straight up and down, not moving forward at all.

Billy noticed that most of the other boats weren't making the nightly run; they just anchored out on the bank. This meant they fished longer and started earlier in the morning. To Billy, who has always made a point of being the first boat on the fishing grounds, this was intolerable, so he started doing the same. The first night was the worst. It broke every rule Billy knew about anchoring. The bottom was deep and there was no shelter. There wasn't even a faint scent of land on the breeze but as darkness fell, he heard the chain and cable of anchorlines winding off winches, and the twinkle of mast lights all around him was reassuring. Billy had become an ocean fisherman.

A few years later, Billy "snuck around the corner" through Scott Channel to the west coast of Vancouver Island. There, *Twilight Rock* went back and forth until the other fishermen teased that he was "wearing a groove" from Hansen Lagoon to Top Knot below Sea Otter Cove. This was nothing like fishing the inlets; an autopilot did most of the steering. Instead of threading his hooks carefully along rocky inlet walls, and veering in and out among reefs, Billy picks a depth, sets his gear and goes straight ahead for hours.

As always, he spends his time keeping his hooks sharp, spoons polished and the legs of the hootchies straight, but fishing the west coast is monotonous. The days are long — up at four and to bed at eleven — so to stay alert, Billy and the other fishermen spend a great deal of time on the radio. They discuss the old days, the future, Fisheries' latest policies, the bite and what's on the stove. There is very little time to actually get together, but they gather on the radio, each group on its own channel, and talk for hours. After a few years off Sea Otter Cove, *Twilight Rock* began appearing elsewhere. The Scott Islands, Brooks Peninsula, Rivers Inlet, Cape St. James — wherever there were fish reported, the little boat was likely to turn up, steadying sail snapping in the breeze.

In 1993, after 21 years on *Twilight Rock*, Billy went into debt for a boat again. This time it was *Ocean Dawn*, an absolutely beautiful classic troller, built for the open waters by second-generation shipwright Morris Gronlund in Vancouver. Father and son have built some of the finest trollers on the coast: *Ocean Sunrise, Ocean Gem, Ocean Troller, Ocean Twilight, Ocean Radiant, Pacific Clipper, Kittywake*

OCEAN DAWN. (PHOTO BY ALEXANDRA MORTON)

V, and *Ocean Fury*. Most are still in fine shape and "I have never heard anyone say a bad word about any of them," Billy declares. Among fishermen that's as good a sales pitch as a boat will ever get.

Highliner

This is what it takes to be a highliner. You have got to be the first boat on the grounds in the morning and the last one to leave at night. You have to keep your lines clean at all times: you can't catch fish if you have jellyfish or junk fish hanging on your hooks. You have got to find the fish before the other guy finds them and when you do find them you have got to make them bite better than the other guy. When the bite is on, you have to work your gear faster than the other guy. And you don't stop to eat as often as the other guy; better yet, you don't eat at all. Most of the time this will give you the little edge you need to beat the hell out of most.

You're always trying to catch more fish than the others, but you've got to try to find out what kind of lure another guy is using without telling him what you are using. And if you do tell him, you learn to lie and you also learn to lie on the phone. "Got a few yesterday but not much today. No good here, too many jellyfish."

When the bite is on and another boat comes by, you go sit in the wheelhouse and hope he doesn't see the poles shaking. Or if he stops and hollers at you, you tell him you haven't had a bite in hours. Or tell him you are just going to pick up and move. Or you tell him you heard there are lots of fish at such and such a place. If you are close to shore, you pick up your gear and go drop the hook and as soon as the other boat is out of sight, you go back fishing.

When you find a killer spoon or plug or hootchie, guard it with your life. I knew guys who would take them to bed with them. When you come in with a big load of fish, you change all your gear and hide all the good stuff and put any old thing out in the stern as if you've been using it. Another trick, if you have a killer hootchie, go to the gear store and buy all they have.

If anyone asks you where you were fishing, tell him some place miles from where you were really fishing. I did that to a guy once and he spent three days looking for me. I was 60 miles away. You have got to make sure your deckhand doesn't go and talk to any other highliner. It's OK if he talks to the low boats. Some guys will fire their deckhands if they talk to anyone.

Sometimes a good way to try and find out what another highliner is using is when you're in port, take some useless spoon or plug or hootchie that you can't catch a damn thing on. Wrap it up in a piece of toilet paper and put it in your pocket and go over to his boat. You look all around and make sure no one else is looking, or if he has visitors you wait till they leave. Then you take this killer out and unwrap it like it was a gem. Well, the other guy will look at it and start going through his gear to see if he has it. This gives you a look at his gear.

If you come in with a real good catch and there are guys watching you unload, get ice, grub and fuel, then tie somewhere that is easy to get out of. Sit there and watch and as soon as they leave their boats to go up town to eat or to the pub for a beer, wait for half an hour, then sneak out and anchor out of sight. That way you can leave in the morning with no one following you.

If you get into good fishing, turn your phone off. Then if someone says I called you and called you but got no answer, you can say without telling a lie that you never heard him. This can backfire, though, if someone was calling to let you know where the bite is on.

Don't get too upset if a certain guy keeps telling you he has more smileys than you have. A lot of the time he is lying. When you are not high boat for a trip you walk around in a sulk. Or you can think up a good excuse. You were in the wrong place, your speed was wrong, the water was too clear, too cold, too hot or there were too many boats. A really good excuse is you got all tangled up when the bite was on and you lost two hours of the best fishing.

Most of these are bullshit, but they do make you feel better. If someone got more big smileys than you, naturally you had a bad roll of perlon [fishing line] and the big ones all broke off. Or the hooks straightened out.

The most common excuse is that there is something wrong with the boat. Don't know what it is, it fished good yesterday, but won't catch anything today. If it fishes like hell tomorrow, you forget this excuse till you're low boat again.

Another thing you *always do* is watch the guy who has more fish than you when he goes to the gear store. You watch to see what kind of hootchies or spoons he is buying. Sometimes this can take a long time because if he sees you watching he will just kind of hover around. A good way to get some action is to duck out the door for a minute. With any luck he'll have the killers lying out on the counter. Most times you won't catch a damn thing on them after all that. You can also look at which boxes of hootchies are almost empty and buy the rest.

Keep your hooks *sharp*.

Keep them *clean* at all times.

Use the *lightest* perlon, lighter than the next guy.

Keep your *leaders straight* at all times.

Try to get more tacks along the hot spot, but never cut anyone off or get in their way.

Don't worry about getting any sleep, because the other guys don't.

When all else fails you can always blame it on your deckhand.

★★★

Anyone who spends a life on the water and in the woods is going to see some strange sights. Some can be accounted for and others remain a mystery. Most have an explanation, but those that don't fall into two general categories — on the Earth and in the sky — and Billy has run across both.

In August of 1952, he was trolling slowly outside the Merry-Go-Round when something sticking out of the water caught his eye. At first he thought it was a sea lion, but as he got closer, more of its body came out of the water, until it stood six feet high. The body was three feet wide, but when it turned sideways, it was only about eight inches thick. A two-foot portion at the top was bent over, like a head. Billy could scarcely believe his eyes. He got within a hundred feet of the animal before it sank straight down. It resembled descriptions of "Cadborosaurus," a "monster" reported elsewhere on the British Columbia coast. Researchers at the University of British Columbia in Vancouver have compiled reports made by people on unidentifiable marine creatures. People have spotted this apparition coastwide and its existence is recorded in Native legends.

One April morning, Billy was returning home from Kingcome Inlet and had just come through Pemphrase Passage. He had one hand on the wheel and the other was holding the radio microphone. He was in mid-conversation with Bobby Lamont, a handlogger, when he noticed a sizeable deadhead floating in the tide line.

Men of the Mainland have an eye for logs. They are always in need of boomsticks, float-logs, firewood logs, lumber logs and crosspieces, so every log is checked out closely. If a log is no good for any of these purposes it lies out there like bait, attracting boats for miles. They swerve towards it, circle like a wolf round a scent, and then dash off again. Billy laughs, "A good log gets more attention out here than a pretty woman."

As he talked, Billy altered course, thinking this looked like a dandy log. It had to be a good size, because it was floating five feet straight out of the water; most deadheads bob just at the surface. But as he got closer, the "log" turned and looked at him. Dropping the microphone in mid-sentence, Billy ran out of the cabin. Whatever it was had large flat eyes, was four to five feet across the neck and its skin formed huge, brown rolls. Running vertically down through the folds were deep, irregular cracks. The creature was startled and rolled over into a dive. As *Twilight Rock* came alongside, the diving animal was stretched along the surface, longer than the boat. Elephant seals grow to 15 feet, and Steller's sea lions are smaller but, curiously, the extinct, 25- to 30-foot Steller's sea *cow* was known as the "bark animal" because deep cracks ran vertically down its neck, resembling the bark of a tree.

Steller's sea cows reportedly became extinct in 1774, 27 years after their discovery off Kamchatka Island in the Bering Sea. However, the researchers at UBC have documented many sightings of the creature Billy saw. In addition, Soviet scientists aboard the whale-catcher ship *Buran* observed a group of animals in 1963 that they thought could be Steller's sea cows, but many consider their observations inaccurate.

Around the same time, Billy was running out to the Burdwood Islands in his speedboat when a large creature surfaced, going the same direction. It had a raised lump on its back that came up about eight inches. It was evidently alarmed by the boat and dove quickly. Billy was unable to swerve fast enough and his boat dropped six inches into the depression the animal left. Within a short time several other people reported a large "log" that would suddenly dive, and for several seconds after disappearing, create a big, single wave ahead of it. One man jigging a cod outside Echo Bay saw the large-eyed "monster" and never fished there again.

In October 1985, Billy spotted a mysterious track in the mud in Simoom Sound. He had an incubation box set up in a small stream in Simoom, trying to enhance the chum salmon run. He had to check the box every two days and had a good trail cleared to it. The track he encountered was on this trail and it was so clear and so strange that he jumped back in his speedboat to get his youngest daughter, Patty. Patty is a keen naturalist and familiar with everything that moves in the woods. He wanted her opinion.

The print was seven inches long and 3½ inches across; it had four toes, with no claws evident. Each toe was 1¾ inches long with one stuck out to the side. It resembled a large beaver track, but it was clear that the creature had been walking on two feet and there was no drag mark indicating a tail. The print was sunk an inch into the mud, and Patty and Billy estimated that whatever made the track must have weighed about a hundred pounds. They never could match the track to any known creature.

That spot in Simoom Sound was a curious place. Occasionally it smelled of anise oil so strongly it brought tears to their eyes.

In June of 1957, a glow was seen in the sky down by Bold Head. Billy, Yvonne and several other fishermen, tied in Yokohama Bay, jumped aboard Billy's boat to investigate. They thought a boat was on fire out in Blackfish Sound. Instead, they witnessed bright red bands of light 200 feet high, stretched out over a half mile. A gentle northwest wind was blowing and the light appeared to be travelling with the wind, heading up into Knight Inlet at about five mph. They watched for half an hour until it faded, without a clue as to what it might have been. The next day a boat brought the paper out and they read that it was an unusual showing of the Northern Lights.

One clear night, Billy spotted a blinking light down by Parson's Bay while gillnetting in Blackfish Sound. The light moved towards him and at first he thought it must be a jet. However, drifting with his engine off, he was surprised when the light passed overhead without a sound and he saw that it was much bigger than a jet. The hair rose on Billy's neck. The thing looked to be 300 feet long and was shaped like a cigar. There were ten big port lights on the side and one big, blinking light in the bottom with a blue tint to it. Whatever it was, it never made a sound as it continued on out of sight. The last he could see of it was the reflection blinking off the water up towards Port Hardy. The entire gillnet fleet saw it too and there was considerable talk about it on the radio for days.

★★★

In 1979, Billy and Yvonne bought 164 acres in Echo Bay. The land had been pre-empted by Louie McKay in 1910 for 25¢ an acre. McKay logged a little of the timber off it, then tried raising foxes and mink. He sold the land to Mark Millington who put it up for sale for $10,000 in 1966. Longing for gardens and something permanent, the Proctors considered buying it then, but figured the price was too high. By 1979, they were tied to the property's beach, with several other families, and decided whatever the price, it was the place for them. They paid $60,000 for their first home together on land.

The Proctor property forms the southeastern border of Echo Bay, including the hills at the head of the bay. It is one of the few pieces of low-lying land — flat land is rare in the steep-sided Mainland inlets. One side overlooks Echo Bay, the other down Cramer Pass. First, they cleared enough of the scrubby timber and brush to build a house and garden. Billy bought a D4 Cat and it took him two years to pull enough stumps to make room for the homestead. He piled the debris and Yvonne and Patty burned it.

The Proctor property, on the southeast side of Echo Bay. (PHOTO BY YVONNE MAXIMCHUK)

140

Jae Proctor and friend, 1971. (COLLECTION OF JAE PROCTOR)

Jae took the job of running the Echo Bay store, although she was in her seventies. Bob Martineau owned the store then and he generally picked her up and took her home to her floathouse. Age never dulled Jae's mind and the people of Echo Bay remember her well, leaning out over the Dutch door of her house, smoking. The smoke left a permanent streak of yellow through her hair. Nothing escaped her attention. Every year, when Billy tied his freshly painted boat to the dock, Jae delighted in pointing out the one spot he'd missed. No matter how he tried, there was always one.

When Joanie was ready for grade nine, she decided to attend the high school in Port McNeill. The Echo Bay School only goes through grade seven, and Joanie did grade eight by correspondence, but she loved school and longed for friends. Correspondence provides an excellent education, but without chums it's boring.

So every Monday morning, Billy headed *Twilight Rock* out in all weather with Joanie and any other Mainland kids who wanted to go to the high school. The children spent the week in a dormitory, but it closed on weekends so Billy picked them up on Friday and they came home for the weekend. Each trip took over three hours, one way, so Billy spent 13 hours a week making sure his daughter could go to school. Ray Rossback, who owned the store in Echo Bay at this point, took advantage of Billy's twice-weekly trips to Port McNeill and chartered him for a small fee to pack propane tanks and food. *Twilight Rock* became a freight boat, as well as the free, unofficial schoolboat.

They had many a wild trip in the winter storms of Blackfish Sound. While the boatload of teenagers was often loud and playful, disciplinary action was required only once, when Billy tied an unruly boy to the stern steering wheel to keep him from hurting himself. Billy was content to provide the service, but he was surprised that some families sent their children with him, without even meeting him or checking out his boat. The kids just showed up at the dock. Everyone trusts Billy.

Patty Proctor hated school and chose to stay in Echo Bay, close to the forest she loved. She put tremendous effort into the homestead. When enough land was cleared, she helped mill the lumber for the house with an Alaska mill and stacked it to dry in the first building on the property: the woodshed. When Billy returned from fishing, they sank the posts and began the construction of the house. They milled the wood with an eye for the inherent beauty of each piece and, as they built, they selected the boards based on their colour and pattern. The result is a richly hued interior of yew, alder, fir, spruce, and red and yellow cedar. Naturally curved cedar knees support the ceiling beams.

The spacious, bright kitchen opens into the dining room where Billy built a large, heavy, round dining table. The living room is a large open space off the dining room. There are no walls, so the space is big enough to host gatherings of the entire community. The floor is an intricate pattern of inlaid wood, and a huge stove keeps the place cosy.

In the attic Billy assembled a museum. He is an avid bottle collector, and there are rows of old bottles, all sorts of equipment and ancient Native artifacts that he has found on beaches and in his garden.

Later, Patty, and Joanie, with her husband Phil, built their own houses on the homestead. Yvonne and Patty fenced off a large garden with a nine-foot-high picket fence. They enriched the soil with buckets of kelp, starfish and "bunny beans" from Patty's rabbits. Despite regular raids from deer, bears, Steller's jays and migratory birds, the garden produces copious yields of food, especially strawberries. Yvonne preserves huge quantities of delicious strawberries, raspberries, loganberries, gooseberries, tayberries and black caps. She also raises chickens and offers their eggs for sale. The homestead provides sanctuary to does with their fawns, and some of the biggest bucks on the island. A few are so tame they eat out of Billy's hand. The cleared area has been increased and over 75 species of migrating birds have used the Proctors' patch of open ground to rest.

In a wilderness where most wives plead with their husbands to move to town, Yvonne stands out. Billy's fishing and logging

Neighbours help to put a new tin roof on the Proctors' house. (PHOTO BY ALEXANDRA MORTON)

meant that she has been on her own most of the time. While she wished he'd been home more for the children, the time alone suited her fiercely independent nature. Some years, he estimates, he was away 340 days a year, though he was home nights when he logged. Yvonne raised the two girls largely on her own and kept the place intact. Speedboats were never to her liking, so she moves about in a beautiful, robin's egg blue Davidson rowboat. Every mail day the "Blue Streak" glides to and from the post office, no matter what the weather.

A true Mainlander, Yvonne keeps a five-year supply of wood in the shed and she is there to care for her daughters' livestock, pets and children. As well, she works at the school, keeping it clean and well maintained. Her dry wit has startled many a newcomer who doesn't know whether to laugh or cry. It is not easy for Yvonne to live in a place where friends, family and neighbours steadily drain away. There are very few family homesteads left on this coast and hers is unique, with three generations thriving on it until 1997, when Joanie and her family left so that her oldest son could go to high school.

Yvonne moving sawdust from the sawmill for Patty's horse's stall. (PHOTO BY ALEXANDRA MORTON)

Yvonne in the "Blue Streak," dog Pal in the bow. (PHOTO BY ALEXANDRA MORTON)

The Proctors' place is the only home in the archipelago with spacious grounds, and they host the two best-attended events of the year: Easter and Halloween. On Halloween, residents and friends converge. Billy takes the children around the neighbourhood in his boat, trick or treating. Then everyone gathers for a bonfire, fireworks and a potluck dinner. Fresh prawns, fried clams, baked salmon, roast venison, pies, braided loaves of bread and other delicacies crowd their table. All the Proctors seem to have a streak of pyromania in their blood and Billy puts on a dazzling fireworks display every Halloween. Of course, everyone best remembers the time the whole box caught fire at once. We dispersed like a flock of starlings as fireworks sizzled across the ground in reds, golds and oranges.

In the spring, Easter eggs are hidden throughout the property and children race the ravens to collect them. The big black birds wing their way into the woods, brightly coloured eggs wedged in their beaks, children shrieking after them.

★★★

Neighbours arriving at the Proctors' place for Easter. (PHOTO BY ALEXANDRA MORTON)

The Easter egg hunt. (PHOTO BY ALEXANDRA MORTON)

The trolling season used to open February 1 and stay open through December 1. However, there weren't enough fish around in February to make any money, so Billy always waited to start his season on April 15 in Knight Inlet. Knight Inlet is a spectacular one hundred miles of steep mountains dropping straight down to the water. At the end of March, and into early April, small fish, oolichans, swim up Knight Inlet to spawn in the two rivers at the head of the inlet, the clear, sparkling Franklin and the deep, powerful Klinaklini. Oolichans are so rich in oil First Nations people burned them as a winter source of light. They also made "grease" from them, a main item of their diet and trade.

Once you eat an oolichan, you crave another the rest of your life, but humans aren't the only ones craving the nourishing little fish. Sea lions, porpoises, dolphins, grizzly bears, eagles, gulls, killer whales, seals and spring salmon all gather at the head of Knight Inlet to feast. Oolichans surge into the rivers at high tide. They tuck themselves in behind the round, multi-coloured river rocks and when the moment is right, attach their tiny eggs to the stones. Enormous grizzly footprints appear in the wet sand magically as

Heading up Kingcome Inlet in search of oolichans. (PHOTO BY ALEXANDRA MORTON)

147

the fish arrive and hundreds of eagles flock to end their winters of near starvation.

The salmon that travel to the head of Knight Inlet in spring are there just to feed, not to spawn. The inlet attracts salmon from the entire south coast and it was these big fish that Billy was after. The next-best-tasting food to an oolichan is a salmon that has been feeding on them.

The glacier in Knight Inlet comes right down to the water so Billy took his boat alongside and chopped ice straight into his hold. Because there was no buyer in Knight Inlet, he had to keep the fish cool. He sold his catch to Dan Sutherland in Simoom Sound every ten days. "It was sure a good life," he says now, more than a little sadly. He would fish Knight until too many other boats showed up, then he would move to Kingcome Inlet and Wakeman Sound. He stayed there until June 20, then returned to Blackfish Sound until the end of the season.

In the late 1940s and '50s everyone fished coho until October 15, but all those late runs have been wiped out, so by the 1960s there

Billy catching oolichans in the Franklin River, head of Knight Inlet. (Photo by Alexandra Morton)

Bald eagle at the oolichan run in Knight Inlet. (PHOTO BY ALEXANDRA MORTON)

were no fish to catch after September 15. Fishing chums could extend a season because chums don't arrive at their rivers until fall, but trollers have problems catching chum salmon; they are more of a net fish. Billy never trolled much for chums. Spring salmon and coho were the trollers' mainstays and of those two, Billy has always liked fishing springs best.

Spring salmon are the most versatile of our salmon. By this I mean that they feed on many different things and they go to many different places. The other species of salmon follow the same migration route, year after year, feeding on the same thing. Sockeye mature at three, four, or five years of age; chum mature at three, four, or five years of age; pinks mature at two, and coho mature at three years of age with the odd one at four years. Springs mature at two, three, four, five, six, seven, or eight years of age and there have been reports of ten year olds with weights up to 125 pounds. A spring salmon returns to spawn at the same age its parents did. White springs only spawn in glacial rivers, like the ones that flow into Knight, Bute and Kingcome inlets.

There are two types of springs: stream and ocean. The stream-type stay in the rivers of their birth for one year. Then they go all the way to the Gulf of Alaska where they feed on the big schools of smelt-like sand lance that live in the North Pacific. The ocean-type springs leave the river within 60 days after coming out of the gravel. When they go to sea they don't go far. Most of them just play and feed within 50 miles of their home river. None of the other salmon species stay around their home rivers like the ocean-type springs do. A few of them will wander farther, but they stay in inside waters. These young ocean-type springs we call "feeder" springs.

Feeder springs are opportunistic feeders. They will eat shrimp, prawns, worms, sand worms that come out at night, shiners, little cod of any kind, herring, sand lance, the slender tube-snouts and oolichans. These ocean-type springs have nursery areas where they stay and feed until they are a year or so old and about 18 inches long. When they leave the nursery area, they roam around up to the head of the inlets, feeding on spawning oolichans and herring. After the spawn the springs drift back down with the herring into bays and channels. There is a time

Landing a "smiley" — a big spring. (PHOTO BY ALEXANDRA MORTON)

when the ocean springs disappear, from July to October, and then they start the cycle all over again. I think they go down deep while the surface water is warmest. When we catch these fish during winter we call them winter springs.

The stream-type springs start entering their rivers in May, peak by the end of June and are all in by the end of July. Ocean springs start into the rivers in late August, peak by the end of September and are all in by the end of October.

When I was younger I could outfish anyone on spring salmon. It seemed like I could will them to bite my spoons. I have done it many times. I used to be able to think like a spring salmon — I would know where they were most of the time. I would go to where I thought they were and most times I would get some. If I didn't get a bite right away, I would start to talk to them. I would talk real nice and when I got the first one on board, I would stroke it and tell it how beautiful it was. If fishing was slow, I would do this to each one I caught. I was always very gentle with them. I never looked at a fish and saw dollars. I always look at them as a beautiful creature. I have admired thousands of them after 50 years of fishing.

My philosophy is: if we stop and appreciate whatever we are after, it doesn't matter if it's lingcod or sockeye or springs, and just don't take them for granted, we will be rewarded with a good catch.

The five species of salmon on the B.C. coast have been given many names. The chum salmon is widely called the dog salmon, because it develops long curved teeth at spawning time that resemble the canines of a dog. Pinks are also known as humpies, due to the males' hump at spawning time, and slime balls due to their prodigious production of protective bodily slime. Sockeye are simply socks. Coho are called silvers in the United States, and when they are immature they're called bluebacks in B.C. Chinook have the longest list of names. Mainlanders call them springs, Americans call them kings. If they are over 30 pounds sport fishermen call them tyees; if over 12 pounds, dressed, commercial fishermen call them smileys. Young spring salmon are shakers,

All five species of Pacific salmon, caught in one pull off Triangle Island. Top to bottom: spring, chum, coho, sockeye, pink. (PHOTO BY ALEXANDRA MORTON)

grilse or feeders. Some individual male coho and springs mature a year earlier than the rest of their age class and they are called jacks. When salmon hatch they are called alevin. After they lose their egg-sac bellies they are fry, until they enter the seawater, when they are called smolts.

In 1979, Billy pushed for a closure that changed his way of life. He didn't want to give up a fishing area and didn't realize it would be for good, but he simply couldn't let the last spring salmon be pulled out of Kingcome Inlet.

An inlet is a good place to fish, because it is narrow and funnels the fish into pockets along the shore. After many years of fishing the inlets, Billy knew where to find most of these pockets of spring salmon. He followed the fish and learned to tell the stocks apart by the way they looked. Some springs are bullet-nosed, some dish-faced; they have marbled, pink, red or white flesh. Some are deep bodied, others more streamlined; some a deep bronze, others with the odd little yellow patch. Fishing around home was a very pleasant way of life and he was making a good living doing it, but he wasn't the only one.

The waters between Kingcome Inlet and Queen Charlotte Strait are clearly an area where immature springs come to feed. It is a nursery. If this nursery area is fished too hard, springs from all over Area 12 will go missing. While he hated to face the reality of it, Billy knew the only answer was to close the area to give the fish a chance. He contacted Fisheries and they agreed. Unfortunately, while they banned the commercial fishery, they allowed sport fishing to grow unchecked in the same waters. The lodge owners said they couldn't live with a closure, but could the fish live without one?

A lot of people have asked me what a fish nursery is. Well, here is how a nursery works. First, it is in a very special location. Number one, it has to have good, clean water. Number two, it has to have lots of feed. Number three, it has to have a bit of tide, but not too much. Number four, the water has to be deep.

Clean water is very important because it has a lot of oxygen. Feed is important because when I say it's a good nursery for salmon, that means it is also a nursery for other sea life. This includes prawns, herring, crabs, and the list can go on for a lot of little critters. What makes a nursery work is everything living in it relying on one another for food. The chinooks feed on baby shrimp and prawns and herring larvae.

A nursery needs a bit of tide to move the food around, but not so much that it all washes out to sea. Deep water is important, mainly because shrimp and prawns like deep water and herring go down deep in the daylight hours.

The reason Greenway Sound and Sutlej Channel below Kingcome form the main nursery for the Broughton Archipelago and Area 12 is its location. It's where shrimp, prawns and the herring larvae from the vast schools that spawn in Kingcome and Wakeman come drifting down in May, just as the salmon smolts are coming out of the rivers.

I started to fish the waters around the Broughton Archipelago in 1951. Back then, Greenway Sound and Sutlej Channel were so full of small springs that it was impossible to keep them off our hooks. Consequently, we stayed away from those areas. In

1966, there were a lot of new boats that came to fish springs. They went into the nurseries and were killing a lot of small springs to get a few big ones.

In May of 1966 I called the Department of Fisheries and Oceans and made a proposal that the waters of Greenway and Sutlej be closed to commercial fishing. They closed them in February 1968. It did help the runs of springs for a time, but since 1991 the springs have gone to nil.

While a commercial salmon boat generally gets more fish per day, per boat, sport gear is much lighter and can therefore be more effective. The small recreational fisherman's boat can easily get into every fishy nook and cranny, and the growing numbers of them must be considered. The number of sport boats dedicated to fishing Kingcome Inlet grew every year. Then in 1987, a large lodge moved into Kingcome with 14 boats. This may have been the last straw for the Kingcome spring salmon, although other factors probably contributed as well. The stock crashed; the nursery area was never really protected at all. Most of the lodges had to close or move a few years later, because there weren't enough fish left.

It is impossible for Billy to feel that the commercial fishermen's sacrifice did any good at all. As the number of big charter boats and commercial sport-fishing lodges increases, it seems clear some kind of control must be exerted over them. There have to be more closed areas, quotas and sensible rules.

The way it is now, a sport fisherman, if he's in the Gulf of Georgia and can go out every day, can catch 720 coho a year. That's too many. When you stop and think that if I shake off a coho, and there's 45 sport fishermen there that can keep that same coho, it doesn't make sense. We're trying to build the stocks up.

The deadliest ones are the big sport-fishing charter boats that follow the fish right from Cape Caution all the way down through areas long closed for commercial boats. DFO has got to extend the boundaries. Sport fishermen can go right up into the rivers. I've seen them with my own eyes trying to hook big coho right out of Charles Creek, right out of the river. Even if the rivers are closed, they can go up to the high-water mark.

Billy can barely contain his anger and disgust at the covers of sport-fishing magazines showing smiling "sportsmen" molesting spawning salmon. It goes against every bit of common sense and decency he has.

The *B.C. Sports Fisherman* keeps publishing pictures on their covers of men standing in rivers holding up salmon with eggs running out of them. That stuff has got to stop. Those guys should not be proud of themselves for doing that.

Billy was invited to join several helicopter fishing trips and while he refused to fish, he went for the ride. He respects everyone's desire to fish, but he was aghast to see men stumbling back and forth in the riffles where salmon had just laid their eggs. The guides argued the gravel would protect the eggs, but freshly dug redds or nests contain loose gravel that shifts and compacts underfoot. Eggs are crushed. Billy was sickened at the sight of fish in the process of spawning being hooked and "played." Does that exhausted fish go back and finish spawning? Is it still capable? No one knew, no one cared.

"There are so many things," Billy will say, in the course of most conversations on fishing. It wasn't just sport fishermen and commercial fishermen depleting the stocks. But what could a guy do?

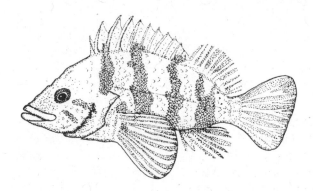

Chapter Eight

God made the old world lovely
He roofed it with the sky,
He ribboned it with rivers
And piled mountains high.
He planted it with roses
That nod and smile and glow,
God made the world lovely
And we must keep it so.

BILLY PROCTOR HAS seen a lot of changes.

Nineteen fifty-seven was a big year for coho in Kingcome. There were 36 trollers there and I had lots of days with over a hundred big coho. In 1968 it was the same, but after that, they logged the Atlatzi River six miles up and that was the end of coho in Kingcome. It was the same thing in Wakeman. They logged the Atwaykellesse River 12 miles from the mouth and the Wahpeeto River at 15 miles and that was the end of the big runs of springs and coho in Wakeman.

Devereux Creek in Knight Inlet is a major coho and spring river and it was logged bare as well. The Ahnuhati is the only big spring and coho river left. They have only logged the mouth. So far.

Bill Macleod was the Fisheries patrolman for the Adams River and Port Neville. He also worked around Kingcome and Wakeman on herring. Macleod and his wife, Frances, lived in a floathouse in Scott Cove, near Echo Bay, and had a boat called *Angelic Isles*. One day in 1978, Macleod and Proctor were talking about how some of the rivers in the area were losing their fish. They needed to be cleaned up and restocked with coho.

A few days later Macleod went into the Sullivan Bay post office. Sullivan Bay is a community smaller than Echo Bay on Broughton Island. In summer, it attracts wealthy yachtsmen, many of whom keep expensive modern floating homes there, some with helicopters on their roofs. One of these summer residents approached Macleod and demanded, "Why don't you do something about the coho in this area?" He liked to fish coho in Wells Pass and like all fishermen, he was finding fewer fish every year.

Macleod was struck by the close timing of this conversation and the one he'd just had with Proctor and he told the man, "We need a hatchery somewhere and we need money."

To Macleod's surprise the man simply asked, "How much?"

Afraid to hesitate, Macleod picked, "$50,000," out of the blue.

The American man on the dock in Sullivan Bay pulled out his chequebook and wrote a cheque for $50,000. Handing it to Macleod he said, "I don't want to be named and I don't want any of it back, but I want you to put coho back in these rivers."

Macleod asked Proctor and several others to work with him on the project and they decided Scott Cove would be a good place to build a coho hatchery. Scott Cove, where Jae had eaten her Christmas can of beans, was home to a Whonnock logging camp (now Interfor). Most importantly, it has good water for raising coho. Scott Cove creek used to have a run of several thousand coho, but by the late 1970s fewer than 50 fish were returning annually. Siting the hatchery in a logging camp meant there would be plenty of electricity available from the camp's generators.

Gary Ordano, a logger at the time, lives and works in Scott Cove. Noticing the declining salmon population, he had already taken it upon himself to clean up the lake above the dam. The dam, built in 1918, was 20 feet square, made of two-foot cedar timbers, and raised the lake 17 feet. When the lake was half filled with logs, they lifted the dam with a steam donkey and shoved the logs down a flume to the ocean. The fall the dam was built, 10,000 coho and 3,000 chum were reported dead at the mouth of the creek. The old dam and collapsing flume were still creating a barrier so dense Ordano didn't see how a salmon could possibly get through. He used his skidder to pull as much wood as possible out of the creek. Now all that was needed was fish.

Whonnock donated land for the hatchery building and cut the lumber on their mill using their timber. Stuart Marshal, a

Logging debris in Scott Cove creek. (PHOTO BY ALEXANDRA MORTON)

Stream cleaning in the Scott Cove system: Billy with Eric Nelson. (PHOTO BY ALEXANDRA MORTON)

renowned Sointula watercolour painter, split the shakes and Robby Boise, from Mitchell Bay, did the construction.

We went to DFO and asked them what we needed. They told us where we could get all the tanks, pipe and stuff and when we had done everything, we needed some fish. There were only about 30 spawners, total, in the river, so we didn't want to take them for broodstock. DFO gave us permission to trap fry from nearby places — Viner Sound, Shoal Harbour, Gilford Creek and Embly Lagoon. We got 16,000 fry, put them in the hatchery and fed them till they were about four inches long, to imprint them on Scott Cove water. That way, they would come back to spawn in Scott Cove and not the rivers where they had been spawned. It takes coho three to four years to mature so we had to do that for three years, to get a run coming back every year.

In those first three years we had our ups and downs. We lost our pipeline in a big flood and we could see we needed a better one, so Bill Macleod phoned the guy that gave us the $50,000 and told him we needed a new pipeline. He asked how much it would cost and Bill said $10,000. The guy said it will be in your bank tomorrow. So we put in the pipeline that is still there.

Once we got runs coming back, we had to pay back all the rivers we took fry from. So, for the second three years, we put fish back in Viner, Shoal, Gilford and Embly. Then we started to stock other rivers. We put fry in Cockatrice Bay, Kenneth River, Sullivan Bay, Charles Creek and kept building up Scott Cove too.

Now we take the broodstock out of Scott Cove and hold them in tanks till they're ripe. Then we take the eggs, put them in the shallow incubating heath trays and when they hatch, we feed them until they are about 2½ grams. Then we fly them out to the rivers with a helicopter. The ones we put back in Scott Cove, we truck up to the creeks that drain into the lakes above Scott Cove creek. We have built up the run in Scott Cove to around 4,000 spawners.

The hatchery depends on the community to help catch the broodstock. Every high tide for weeks, Billy wades chest deep into the frothing creek, leans as far forward as he dares, slides a dipnet beneath boulders and catches a few beautiful silver coho. Weighing up to 16 pounds, each fish is placed in a tube, head down and pulled across the creek and up the bank on a clothesline. As soon as the tube is across, volunteers relay-race it down the hillside, each standing 200 feet from the next.

The trail is generally knee deep in mud so we careen about through a tangle of roots and bear droppings, mindful not to knock our precious cargo. Breathlessly we pant, "It's a boy," or "It's a girl," as we hand the fish off to the next runner to get it into the right tank. The fish must reach the hatchery as soon as possible, because there is not enough oxygen in the tube to sustain it for long. After years of practice we get the fish into the hatchery in about 2½ minutes!

As soon as a human chooses which fish mate together, that population of fish begins a genetic drift away from the original stock. The genes of each population of salmon have been fine-

160

Billy catching broodstock in Scott Cove creek. (PHOTO BY ALEXANDRA MORTON)

tuned to the creek where it was spawned. It is very difficult to take salmon from one river and get them to spawn in another, because each salmon fits its river like a key to a lock. There are many types of rivers — long, steep, cold, glacial, slow, fast, deep, wide — and there are different salmon stocks for each. Big hatcheries have had a dubious impact on wild populations by overwhelming and thus destroying natural genetic blends. Too often, hatcheries are built to substitute for the destruction of river habitat. This is not a solution, only a band-aid, temporarily preventing us from witnessing the extinction of another salmon stock. Take away the hatchery and nothing is left.

Small hatcheries, however, seem able to revive local stocks if the outplanted fish are left to spawn on their own. Charles Creek, for example, once home to a cannery, was given back coho fry from the Scott Cove hatchery. The broodstock of Charles Creek have never been taken into a hatchery. They choose their own mates and are thus recreating the perfect Charles Creek coho, big, vigorous and wild.

An essential ingredient for successfully reinstating salmon to a river is viable habitat. Using a hatchery to avoid habitat work is counter-productive, simply boosting fish numbers artificially for a few years. It is farming rather than enhancement. For a hatchery to be successful, the fish must be re-established to breed on their own. With both a hatchery and habitat work, miracles may happen.

At the Scott Cove hatchery Billy shouldered the responsibility of figuring out when to take the eggs. Spawning is a fatal act for Pacific salmon whether in the wild or in a hatchery. In a hatchery, males and females are separated, because without gravel, the tanks are not a good place for salmon eggs to be laid. They are fertilized artificially and placed in incubating trays. If Billy takes the eggs too soon they aren't ripe enough to be fertilized and so the salmon's life and her thousands of eggs are wasted. If he waits too long the eggs are released uselessly into the tank, unfertilized. Scott Cove coho broodstock ripen slowly over a period of months so it is difficult to discover exactly the right day for the conception of a salmon.

Male salmon, as in many species, live months in a state of readiness to spawn and can fertilize several batches of eggs. To encourage fertilization with the strongest sperm, hatchery workers

Checking salmon eggs in the hatchery. (PHOTO BY ALEXANDRA MORTON)

use several males to provide sperm for each female. The eggs are placed in a bowl and the milky sperm added. Salmon sperm has only a few seconds to penetrate an egg, before contact with water hardens the eggs' outer membrane. Gentle stirring distributes the sperm, then water is added to seal the tiny lives within their eggs.

The eggs are placed in trays and creek water pours over them continuously. Dead eggs are delicately picked out of the trays by hand to prevent fungus from destroying the brood. The baby fish hatch with egg sacs hanging down from their bellies. When they've absorbed the nutrients contained within the sacs and have "buttoned up," the tiny fish are placed in the troughs that once held their parents. They are fed a mixture of fish products and supplements created to give them a healthy start in life. In spring, the community is called on again to help fly the tiny fry to their rivers.

The flyouts are very exciting. The baby fish wriggle actively as they are scooped out of the steel troughs into five-gallon buckets. It is wonderful to know that soon these fish will be darting for cover in a wild stream. The buckets of baby fish are carefully emptied into a large fibreglass box on a platform outside the hatchery. A helicopter swoops in and manoeuvres a huge canvas bucket, hanging from a long line, to just below the box containing the fish. In the roar and wind of the propeller blades, the fish and water are drained into the canvas bucket.

Everyone works quickly because the little fish are rapidly using up their oxygen. When the signal is given, the pilot expertly flies the babies away. Minutes later he lowers the helicopter until the bucket grazes the surface of the creek at a spot carefully chosen for the fry's survival. The pilot releases the bottom of the cloth bucket and the fish are free. They are young enough so that they will imprint on the scent of the new stream, big enough to survive and genetically close enough to the stream's original inhabitants to restock it. The Scott Cove creek has been built up to thousands of fish once again.

★★★

Preparing salmon fry for the flyout. (PHOTO BY ALEXANDRA MORTON)

Helicopter flying the fry out of the hatchery to Scott Cove creek. (PHOTO BY ALEXANDRA MORTON)

In 1986, a fledgling industry dipped its toe into the archipelago and slid in amidst rumours, controversy and plain bad feelings. When the first salmon farm was towed into the Mainland, Billy began to worry and he kept an eye on it.

John and Nadine Ebbel ran one of the early farms for Stolt Sea Farms and they too were concerned about the new industry they were part of. Since Billy is widely known as an expert on fish, John and Nadine visited to ask his advice on where to set up the farms.

While he was suspicious of the idea of farming salmon, Billy lent his expertise. The Ebbels' questions made him feel they were concerned about the impact of the industry on the wild stocks and Billy never could turn away a person asking for help. He pored over charts with the Ebbels. Careful to avoid salmon migration routes, holding and nursery areas, as well as herring spawning sites, clam beds, prime prawn habitat, seal haulouts and more, Billy chose five sites. Stolt Sea Farms trusted Billy's judgment and those are some of their most productive sites.

Then two more companies arrived and chaos set in. Gunshots, previously banned from floating structures, rang out frequently from the fish pens, as seals, Steller's sea lions, sea gulls, mink, otter, herons and other species were killed for trying to eat the farmed fish. The bounty-hunting days had returned. Loud underwater "Acoustic Harassment Devices" were installed to produce sounds so loud they would be painful to marauding seals. These sounds carry for miles, and humpback, Minke whales and killer whales began avoiding the archipelago.

There were rumours of nets being cut to dump tons of dead and diseased fish, people throwing food into pens with no fish to create the appearance of livestock that did not exist, mink and otters being wounded and left to the dogs to be finished off. Billy was even told that just before a company was sold, a disease was introduced to create an epidemic to cover up for the fish that had only existed on paper. The fish farmers were required to advertise each new site in the *North Island Gazette*, the local newspaper, to give people the opportunity to object.

Billy, who had never been to school, began writing letters to the Ministry of Environment, and he encouraged his neighbours to do

Steller's sea lions. (PHOTO BY ROBIN MORTON)

the same. He knew that if a fraction of the rumours he was hearing were true, the farms would destroy the wild fish.

At first, spring salmon were farmed. In an effort to domesticate this wild species, the fish farmers robbed B.C. rivers of valuable broodstock and placed their progeny in pens. They were bred experimentally, creating entire pens of albino spring salmon. Springs, however, did not take well to captivity and so the industry pleaded with the government to permit them to import domesticated Atlantics from Scotland.

Despite warnings from scientists and Norwegian bureaucrats, and ignoring public protest, the federal and provincial governments said go ahead. None of the sites Billy or anyone else objected to were denied. Even the objections of Fisheries officers were ignored. The industry mushroomed as it had in Norway, Scotland and Ireland and the same devastating chain of events replayed here as in those countries.

Suddenly, the coho returning to Scott Cove were sick. They arrived with red oozing sores down their silvery sides. For nine years Billy and the community of Echo Bay had carefully built up the stocks. The hatchery had an exemplary, disease-free history. Now Billy worried over those fish as if they were his children, spending sleepless nights trying to figure out what he had done wrong. Watching them die broke his heart. Billy took one of his fish to a local fish farm to ask the manager if she had ever seen this disease. She said no.

The Department of Fisheries and Oceans was familiar with the disease. They knew it as furunculosis and sent the hatchery an antibiotic, oxytetracycline, to inject in every fish. Each surviving coho was gently lifted out of the troughs and held while a hypodermic needle injected the drug just forward of the dorsal fin. This wasn't what Billy had in mind when the hatchery started, but it was a miracle drug. The sores healed, the fish lived and their eggs were collected. In spring the fry were tested and found to be disease free. DFO doesn't allow diseased fish to be placed from hatcheries into rivers, an excellent policy.

Unfortunately, the same policy doesn't apply to the fish farmers. It wasn't until much later that the salmon farmers came to Billy's homestead and told him that the Atlantic salmon on neighbouring farms had been infected with furunculosis before being put in the archipelago. They later said their insurance wouldn't cover the loss of fish that died in their hatcheries, but it would cover fish that died in seawater. That was why the diseased Atlantic salmon from Scotland

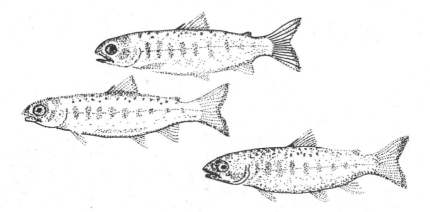

Coho fry. (DRAWING BY ALEXANDRA MORTON)

had been put into pens in the Mainland. Billy was furious that wild salmon had been infected with a disease that may have come from Scotland, and that the farm manager he had approached had refused help while it was her fish that had probably started the epidemic.

This was not an isolated incident. In a year when salmon farms were fighting bacterial kidney disease, the chum salmon had returned to the Mainland as always, jumping in their characteristic semi-circles. But they never arrived on their spawning grounds. The entire Viner Sound stock crashed that year, from 65,000 to mere hundreds, and has never recovered. Billy had to wonder if disease killed them too. Later, another company put fish infected with an antibiotic-resistant disease into Sutlej Channel, part of the chinook nursery Billy had fought to protect. The disease spread rapidly to another farm in Greenway Sound and the young wild spring salmon living in that area vanished too.

DFO recognized that the disease had spread farm fish to farm fish, but refused to acknowledge that it might have spread from farm fish to wild fish. That fall, the beleaguered Scott Cove coho were infected with an antibiotic-resistant disease as well. And the magnificent spring salmon of Kingcome are gone. DFO said it was coincidence — again. But to a man who had watched these fish most of his life, that did not ring true.

A seine and gillnet fishery in Johnstone Strait in August 1993 produced over 5,000 Atlantic salmon. The gillnetters reported that sockeye coming in from the open ocean hit one side of their nets, while the Atlantics heading out to sea hit the other. Fisheries responded by including Atlantic salmon in the annual Sport Fishing Regulations. Instead of seeing the danger of an exotic species of salmon invading the delicately balanced Pacific salmon stocks, they ignored it, and even started to protect the Atlantics by limiting how many people could catch.

Billy couldn't believe his ears when salmon farmers and DFO began telling him the wild salmon were on their way out. Wild salmon feed so many species — birds, other fish, whales, bears, people. How could farm salmon possibly replace the wild salmon in the ecosystems of the Pacific Coast? Without them, death, and extinction of many species, would occur.

Unnatural partners: clear-cut logging above a salmon farm. (PHOTO BY ALEXANDRA MORTON)

Billy has watched the effects of human activity all his life.

When I was a boy, there were a lot of anchovies on the coast, so they started to fish them. Soon there were no anchovies left so they stopped fishing for them. But the funny thing is, the fishers didn't know what happened to them. They said they must have moved away. But I wonder why the anchovies moved as soon as they started to fish for them?

Next came the sardines off California. The sardines would come in, in big schools every year, so they started to fish for them and they got lots. They built more, bigger and better boats and made longer and deeper seines. Soon, like the anchovies, the sardines never showed up one year. Where did they go? Funny how all of a sudden they moved away. Some say it was warm water that made them move away.

Next it was the pilchard on this coast. Huge big schools were all along the coast, but mostly on the west coast of Vancouver Island. Well, they started to fish for them and the pilchard were easy to catch. The boats were small, so they brought up some of the sardine seiners and also built some bigger ones that could pack more and move around faster. More boats needed more fish and to get more fish they needed more time so, like the anchovies and the sardines, the pilchard were soon gone. We don't know why they never showed up one year, but that was the end of the pilchard. Even today someone will say they don't know what happened to the pilchard; it had to be the warm water.

Next was the humpback whale. They came and harpooned them in the inlets all along the coast, and they didn't come back for a long time.

Then it was the herring. They used to fish herring in the wintertime, before they spawned, and then they got bigger boats and deeper seines. Then came sounders and drums and more boats and still bigger boats and deeper seines so they needed more fish and more time to fish them, and they started to fish them in the summertime. Well, they fished a few summers and then one winter there were not many herring to be found. Don't know where they went.

So someone got the idea to use lights to attract herring to the surface. It was called pit-lamping. I watched them from my bay. One night there were 22 boats, all working out in front of my house and they were attracting everything to the lights: octopus, all types of cod, etc. Well, it worked for a while, but soon there was not many that would come to the lights. So they closed down herring fishing on this coast. No one knew where the herring went. They must have died offshore they said, or they moved west. They never came back into many of the bays to spawn. At one time there was about a hundred miles of spawn in Area 12 and then there was only about ten miles. They told me the herring started spawning down so deep that they never fished them out.

There was a lot of herring on the east coast, so some people got the idea to go there, and away they went, boats, seines, drums, pit-lamps and in about five years the herring were gone. Well, this is odd, where did they go? Did they move out to sea, over to Norway, down deep or maybe they died? But they were gone and, people said, not overfished.

Well, the herring did come back to this coast, but it took a long time and many closed seasons. But even now, after 30 years, they are still not coming to spawn in a lot of the areas they used to. Other recent declines include the quillback rockfish. Fifteen years ago you could drop a jigger down just about anywhere in the Mainland and come up with a nice feed for supper. I think they are fished out in the Mainland, almost to the point of no return. No one will ever see rockcod fishing in the Mainland like when I was a kid. They used to get their quota in three or four months; now they don't get it in a year. You would think that would tell them something, but it doesn't.

A lot of people think they own the things on this planet, but they are wrong, because we are just visiting for a short time and then we are gone. We have to remember that everything has its place and everything is there for a reason. Who are we to say that this or that has to go? Everything was here before we came here and I hope that everything will be here after we are gone.

Billy did not have a plan, but he knew it was time for him to do something to save the salmon in his beloved Mainland. It was not only the salmon farms that were a threat, but also the growing number of sport-fishing lodges, the tons of pesticides being sprayed on the hillsides, the draggers with nets so big they remove the entire foodchain, DFO's policy of electroshocking fish to count them in streams, helicopters hovering over spawning salmon and interrupting the fish at the moment of conception, negligent logging practices causing landslides into salmon rivers, and road blasting. Everywhere Billy looked there were problems. He wasn't looking for these problems; they kept coming to him.

A sharp dynamite blast on a rock cut near a salmon stream can kill eggs up to at least 300 metres away. We've proven that in the hatchery. The dryland sort in Scott Cove is over 200 metres away from the hatchery. When they blasted there the eggs went dead in the hatchery immediately, even though we tried to protect them by suspending the egg trays on rubber bands. Twice they've done that and nothing we could do saved those eggs. Imagine what that's like when the eggs are lying on bedrock in a river.

There's times they can blast and never hurt an egg, but the crucial times have got to be respected or no salmon are going to hatch that year. We tried to get them to delay their blasting on the dryland sort, but they wouldn't and we couldn't save those eggs.

It was obvious where all this was heading, but what could one man do? All his life, Billy's greatest ambition had been to be the best fisherman, but now his thoughts were breaking new ground. Second to catching a big spring salmon, Billy's greatest joy was nothing more than a good conversation. Whether standing on a dock in the pouring rain, drifting beside another boat or on the VHF radio, he talked to other people every day of his life. Not content with the pleasantries of a brief exchange, Billy loved to really *talk* about whatever was on his mind. When he realized his world was dying around him, all he knew was to talk about it.

At first he spoke with his neighbours, then he went to meetings, then he called meetings. Usually soft-spoken, he found himself barely able to contain his growing rage when DFO told him diseased Atlantic salmon on wild migration routes were not a problem, when loggers refused to delay blasting by a few weeks to save thousands of salmon eggs, when sport fishermen placed all the blame for the demise of wild salmon on commercial fishermen and when forestry representatives told him pesticides were harmless. He began to boil over. At home, Yvonne heard it all over and over and she encouraged him to get out there and do what he could, before he self-destructed.

Generally, when a big company starts destroying a place, they count on no one having a clear memory of exactly what had existed before their arrival. When they moved into the Mainland, they did not expect any problems from Proctor — fisherman, logger and trapper — but they were wrong. He remembered the events, the lies and the consequences.

They say you've got to trust the experts. Well, in 1957 the experts said DDT wouldn't hurt anything and they sprayed 150,000 acres on the north end of Vancouver Island from airplanes. That year in the Keogh River there were 40,000 coho, but only 300 returned three years later. One guy went down to the bank of the Nimpkish River and shovelled a wheelbarrow load of dead fry out of the river and wheeled them up to the Forestry office. They killed the whole end of the island; they killed the Nimpkish, Keogh, Suquash, Shushartie, Stranby and Nahwitti. They killed them all. There used to be tremendous runs of sockeye and coho in all those rivers. Now they are spraying this area and they're telling us it is safe again. I don't believe them; there's no way I can.

They tell me it's absolutely harmless. If it's harmless, why do they store it in sheds lined with ¾-inch plywood, fibreglassed inside and painted with gelcoat, under lock and key? That sounds like toxic waste to me. And it is.

Chapter Nine

Ecosystems are not only more complex than we think, they're
more complex than we *can* think.

Aldo Leopold, in *A Common Fate*, by Joseph Cone, 1995

WHEN I FIRST encountered Billy Proctor in his red-checked flannel shirt and jeans in 1984, to ask whether whales frequented the Mainland, I began frantically fishing through my pockets for paper and pen. I hadn't expected more than the usual vague reply I had been getting from people up and down the coast. His was more than an answer; it was data.

I fell in love with the Mainland irrevocably that first winter. I followed whales throughout Kingcome Inlet, Tribune Channel and the rest of the archipelago, researching their language. Whenever I saw something curious I went to Billy. Fresh from university, I was used to a different type of teacher, but I recognized Billy as a man who knew my study area better than I ever would. I think my pestering amused him. He'd see me coming and laugh, "What now?" We stood many hours in the near-constant rain discussing an unusual salmon, the latest herring spawn or how he figured periwinkles had been moving increasingly landward throughout his life.

Blackfish

We always called killer whales "blackfish." I never heard the term killer whale before 1966. I'd also never seen a man with long hair and beads around his neck before that year. One day while I was trolling off Bold Head, this kayak came along and asked me if I had seen any killer whales. I didn't know what he was talking about. I had never seen anyone like him in my life. He had hair down to his ass and three strings of beads around his neck.

Then he tried to tell me what a killer whale looked like, with a big fin, and I said, "You mean blackfish." He'd never heard the word.

Killer whales in Johnstone Strait in a multiple spy hop. (PHOTO BY ROBIN MORTON)

A few days later a school of blackfish came along past Bold Head and there was an armada of kayaks following them. Leading the kayaks was a small power boat with a cabin. It was painted all brown and it was real old looking. But what was the most bizarre thing was a guy standing on it, bare naked with long hair blowing in the wind. He was beating his chest and screaming into the wind. I could not believe my eyes. I thought, "My God, what next?"

In September 1986, my husband, Robin, drowned and my four-year-old son Jarret and I were left in our little house on an island. My father phoned to say, "I'm coming to take you home, darling," and that is when I knew I couldn't leave. It was a terrible time, but this was my home. I didn't know for a long time that Billy had lost his father when he was about the age of my son, but I was struck by his knowing what we needed to survive. One day I found five logs tied anonymously to the beach in front of my house, enough firewood for the entire winter.

Billy helps everyone. Every ten days or so he lets it be known he's heading to town. Whoever shows up at his dock in the morning is welcome to ride with him. When we get to Port McNeill we scatter like crows, clutching our shopping lists and children. We have four hours. By 3:00 PM all our groceries, plywood, cement, whatever, has to be aboard and he takes us home again. He never complains about the load and never charges a cent. Blackfish Sound is too rough most winter days for a small boat, so Billy's town trips make life a lot easier for the community. Like his father, Billy has no fear of the sea, and some of the rides are pretty rough.

I'm a dedicated chicken, but I've had many a proud moment when people·in town say, "You're not going home in *this* weather, are you?"

Scared stiff, I love saying, "Yup."

Billy helps people because it's in his nature and because he wants to keep the Echo Bay community alive. He and Yvonne don't want to be the last people here. Most of the communities on the B.C. coast have withered and died. First the big companies pull out,

Loading the neighbours' goods and groceries aboard TWILIGHT ROCK. (PHOTO BY
ALEXANDRA MORTON)

then the schools close, next the post office folds and the last few
lonely souls remain until they are gone too. Although Echo Bay
has shrunk considerably, from about a hundred people when I
arrived, to less than 40, it's still alive and I know Billy and Yvonne
are in part responsible.

In 1989 Billy noticed I wasn't making ends meet and one day he
muttered, "You oughta come deckhanding for me."

I wasn't sure I'd heard him right. "Me?" I asked.

"Sure. It's hard work, but you'll make yourself a bit of money
and you love fishing."

He was right; I was feeding my son and myself on the fish I
caught, but I was terrified at the thought of fishing on the open
ocean. However, it was too much of an adventure to turn down
and I could only think of two questions. Could Jarret come with
me and was it OK with Yvonne? With both answers "Yes," I took
the job.

I figured the man had been on the water his whole life, and so it
was probably a safe bet I'd survive the summer, but I was far from

Alexandra Morton landing a spring. (PHOTO BY BILLY PROCTOR)

convinced. On opening day Billy headed for the Yankee Bank, just east of the Scott Islands off the northern tip of Vancouver Island. As soon as *Twilight Rock* sank her nose into the first open ocean swell, nausea hit.

Jarret and I composed a song about Billy's favourite fishing spot. It went to the tune of "Home on the Range": "Barf, Barf on the Yankee Bank...." It was awful and I wanted to quit. But when we delivered ten days later, the pay cheque made it all worth it and I stuck with it for two full seasons and two partial ones after that. The nausea never went away, but it wasn't debilitating. I pulled fish, cleaned them, tied hundreds of pieces of gear, cooked and cleaned. We ate a lot of fresh fish.

Salmon Sointula Style

Place fillets in a roasting pan or on a cookie sheet with edges.
Sprinkle liberally with garlic powder.
Cover with brown sugar till it is hard to see the pink of the flesh.
Wet thoroughly with soy sauce.
Place in broiler, or oven on high heat.

Baste with the sugar every five minutes at first, then as the sugar caramelizes, baste every three minutes, until the fish flakes apart. The time will vary with the size of the fish.

Enjoy, and it's even better the next day!

Salmon or Halibut Proctor

Place fillets in roasting pan.

Cover in mayonnaise with a bit of soy sauce and garlic powder mixed in it.

Put in oven at 350 degrees. Check often for doneness and remove as soon as the fish starts to flake.

It was obvious Billy loves fish. You can tell a lot by the way a person holds a fish. Some are disgusted, holding them awkwardly away from their bodies to keep contact to a minimum. Billy cradles them, touching each one gently. "What a beautiful fish," he says, a hundred times a season. Does it matter if a fish dies cruelly or with respect? I think so.

Billy is very strict about keeping every bit of garbage on the boat, from old fishing line to plastic bags. He even collects what he can off the beaches. I was dismayed by the amount of garbage floating around the fleet. Some crews were throwing everything overboard. The albatrosses and sooty shearwaters bobbed among margarine containers and baloney wrappers. The amount of refuse we made, just the three of us on each ten-day trip, made me think about how much was going overboard. If you respect life, you have to respect its habitat and that becomes a way of life. It is essential we learn to live in Earth's ecosystems rather than despoiling each one in turn.

Another thing Billy was strict about was being the first boat out of the anchorage, if we were in an anchorage at all. Sometimes he dropped the anchor in what looked like the middle of the ocean to me. I couldn't sleep those nights, although Billy's thunderous snores made it clear he was not concerned.

Morning comes early on the central coast of British Columbia. The dreaded sound of the anchor winch started at 4:30 AM, before even the first hint of daybreak, and that anchor didn't touch bottom again until about 11:30 PM. The thought of sleep swirled deliciously through my brain all day, every day, like melting chocolate. I had to take naps, but Billy never did. "Might miss the bite."

The night before a storm Billy made sure to anchor near a good beach so he could explore it the next day. Jarret did a week's worth of running as soon as his feet touched the sand and we saw some incredible places: ancient First Nations middens, bogs full of frogs, long sandy beaches. Rowing to and from the beaches was often as memorable as the beach itself. As careful as he is elsewhere, Billy is a maniac in a rowboat. He'd row over reefs in a huge swell. A wave brought us down on one, splitting the hull. I had to hold my hand over the geyser to keep us from swamping.

Another time he started the tiny boat surfing towards a dark, foaming cave. When we got to the narrow entrance I lunged for the cliff and hung on. There was no way I was going in there. So while Jarret and I waited, Billy swooshed in. As I pondered our fate if he didn't return, he came out, laughing so hard he could barely row. I felt sorry for Jae and all the moments she must have thought her boy was lost.

The littlest deckhand: Jarret Morton with a big white spring. (PHOTO BY ALEXANDRA MORTON)

180

Jae Proctor's former floathouse. (PHOTO BY ALEXANDRA MORTON)

Fishing with Billy was a ride into the soul of the coast. I met fishing families and fishbuyers, explored fishing towns and fishing grounds. I breathed, ate, was covered in and depended on fish. Without fish, I began to understand, the coast would die.

With my first season's pay cheque I bought the only home I could afford, Jae's derelict floathouse. Jae Proctor passed away the fall I arrived; I never met her. The roof now leaked, otters lived in it and the ancient building had been stripped of most of its inside walls, the plumbing and the chimneys.

The first job was clearly a new roof, but how? Elsewhere, I would have spent thousands of dollars, but here my neighbours showed up. It was a wet, cold January day. I made a batch of chocolate chip cookies, which the dogs ate. Despite this, there were people all over my roof hammering, laughing and giving me a hard time for making them suffer.

Billy was there (it was his idea), and so was Bill Ford, a giant of a man. He arrived in the Mainland in a kayak and became a cod fisherman. One summer day Bill was out fishing in his 27-foot dory when a young Japanese tourist spied him from a whale-watching boat. She found a way to meet the fisherman and soon Bill was being outfished by his petite wife, Hiromi. They have two daughters, Anna and little Beth. Chris Bennett pounded nails alongside Bill. Chris had just finished his own roof. He came to the Mainland as a fishing guide, then a few years later he built a beautiful lodge. Billy's daughter, Patty, and artist Yvonne Maximchuk were there as well. In three days, I had a snug, shingle roof.

Strangely, it has become clear that the government doesn't want people living out here any more. When I applied for a foreshore lease to tie my new home to the shore, they said no.

After decades when floating communities flourished on this coast, the federal government sent a Memorandum of Understanding to the provincial government. There would be no foreshore leases for homes. They would only grant leases for tying up log booms, salmon farms and moorage for tourists. In the stroke of an anonymous pen, a traditional way of life on the B.C. coast was outlawed.

Neighbours help to put a new roof on Alexandra's house. L. to r.: Bill Ford, Billy Proctor, Yvonne Maximchuk, Chris Bennett, Patty Proctor. (PHOTO BY ALEXANDRA MORTON)

Crown Lands, a branch of the Ministry of Environment, began flying over people's homes, photographing them and then sending letters stating that while a lease was required to live here, we couldn't have one. Police boats said no one could pull a drifting log home for firewood, even though according to regulations, debris can be salvaged. A park was created in the archipelago which would allow fishing lodges, with fish farms on the borders, and tourist moorage, but the floathomes had to go. People who were willing to build sewage containment, pay leases and abide by the rules were told to leave.

No one would argue that a floathouse has no impact on the environment, but compared to the suffocating mat of bark that log booms shed on the sea floor, the chemicals, faeces and disease wafting out of fish farms and the aftermath of hundreds of tourists, each trying to catch their limit of fish, the effect of one home is so minute it would be hard to measure. People began commenting on how similar this was to the land clearances of Scotland. When rules become impossible to obey, people have no choice; they just go on with their lives.

I decided to move ashore; Billy was trying to sell off a bit of land to a few neighbours. While the fellow at Crown Lands who had denied me a foreshore lease said my son would be grown and gone before he would approve the subdivision of Billy's land, it seemed the only option. At least the answer wasn't a flat no. In the end, he was right. My son moved to town to finish high school before the subdivision came through. It took seven years.

I wanted to move Jae's old house back ashore and Billy accepted the challenge. This time the slope was steeper than in Freshwater Bay. When he got the house pulled part way up, a splice in the cable snagged against the block and the cables separated. The house slid back down to the beach and hit hard. On another pull the tremendous weight caused a block to fly apart and down she went again, laying the floor joists over more each time and twisting the floor out of shape.

The house spent the night on the beach and the tide came in, washing away a mess of broken jars of pickled beets and salmon. I was a wreck. Worried that someone would get killed I suggested we buck

Jae's former house going up onto Alexandra's property. (PHOTO BY ALEXANDRA MORTON)

the house up for firewood. Billy laughed and assured me that it wasn't that bad. I noticed, however, that he did ask me to go and get help, in the form of Jack Scott. Jack was in his seventies, a gyppo logger from way back who'd moved more buildings than he could remember. He lived around the corner in Shoal Harbour in a floathouse.

"Hang on, sweetie, I'll be right there," Jack bellowed as he tugged on his boots. He called all the women sweetie.

Most of the windows broke and some beams shattered, but my house finally came up the hill, complaining every inch of the way. When Billy began the move he called my house the little shack, but by the end he was wondering if he could move "the bitch." But he did and honeysuckle is starting to creep up her walls again. Billy swears he is never moving it again.

The first time I met Jack Scott was at Minstrel Island in December 1944. Mum and I were waiting for the boat to go to Vancouver and Jack was sitting there on the dock with a jug of rum. He called me over and said, "Hey matey, would you like a sip of rum, lad?"

I said, "No thanks."

Jack said, "Ah, lad, you don't know what you are missing."
That was the start of a lifelong friendship.

Jack was a good logger and well liked. He was good at just about anything he put his mind to. He was a good boom man. I don't think I ever saw anyone better at running around on logs; give him a pike pole and he'd run out on the slipperiest logs. Jack loved to tow anything — day or night, it never mattered to him.

Jack loved parties and potlucks, telling stories and jokes. He and his wife Yvonne floated around the dance floor.

Jack got the school Christmas tree every year. He loved clams, and he shucked them he sliced out the muscle and ate it raw with a bit of special sauce. Though he drank hard for years, he joined Alcoholics Anonymous and spent the last decades of his life sober. But "sober" never really described Jack — he was so quick to laugh. When I asked him how he'd managed to marry a woman as beautiful as his wife Yvonne, he replied, "I married her before she

Jack Scott bringing the Christmas tree to the Echo Bay Community Hall for the Christmas concert. (PHOTO BY ALEXANDRA MORTON)

knew what she was doing." Theirs was the best marriage I have ever seen. Jack died in 1994.

Every spring the community shrinks a bit only to grow again in the fall. I met Dave and Cory Parker pushing their float across Blackfish Sound. As I pulled alongside in amazement, there was Dave pounding the float together with driftbolts, while Cory pushed the float with a small, open speedboat. A tiny, angelic daughter, Traci, was nestled in her arms.

"Where are you going?" I called across the water.

Dave looked up as if pounding driftbolts in the middle of Blackfish Sound was the most natural thing in the world and replied, "Over there," his long arm pointing toward the Broughton Archipelago.

They had no radio and were so low to the water they probably would not show up on another boat's radar. I was concerned they might be hit by a cruise ship in the drifting fog, so I alerted Vancouver Traffic to their passage. All the vessels transitting Blackfish Sound would now know to look out for them. They thought they were alone and I thought my call was all that was protecting them, but Al Munro kept them in sight as he set his prawn gear and Billy's daughter, Joanie, watched their progress from a fish farm where she was working. They hadn't even crossed the sound yet and already they had been taken into the safety net of this community.

Tim Motchman first paddled into the Mainland in a little kayak. Raised in Africa, England and the interior of B.C., Tim found his place in the world here. Soon he bought a tiny sailboat, then one slightly larger and he began carving the wildlife around him. Every Sunday Tim took my son out, in the spirit of the Big Brother program. As Tim learned how to handle wood and his knives, his carvings came to life.

Then he met Kate Pinsonneault in Sointula. While single, Tim loved teasing the rest of us about the things we put up with to raise children and dogs. Kate had two daughters, Karen and Alida, and a massive dog, and soon they had a daughter together, Elena. Tim clearly needed a bigger boat. In the winter of 1997-'98 Tim and Kate ran the Echo Bay store with their boat, *Sea Horse*, tied to the dock, its tiny wind generator whirring away. Tim's carvings are in demand throughout the province and beyond.

Glen and Margaret Neidrauer bought land next to me and moved their floathouse ashore. They are among the busiest people I have ever known, fishing for prawns, working for DFO on patrol, homesteading, putting barrels under floathouses to keep them from sinking. Glen has volunteered hundreds of hours at the Scott Cove hatchery as president, vice-president and worker. Glen knows the watersheds of the Mainland well, walking them every fall counting fish. He too has become deeply concerned about the decline in salmon and the difficulties in getting DFO to understand what he is witnessing.

Claudia Maas, a stone carver, is from Germany and Pierre Alarie is from Quebec. They found their way to the Mainland tree planting, and decided this was home. Claudia now runs the hatchery, her son Lucas usually on her back as she picks the eggs, feeds the fish and keeps everything clean and running smoothly.

Bob and Nancy Richter bought the Echo Bay store in 1980. Nancy was a computer hardware and software installer and Bob sold video equipment, and they found Echo Bay while vacationing on their boat *Freedom II*. They loved the bay at first sight and when they discovered the store was for sale they decided to live their dream. Echo Bay had become a sport-fishing resort, but the post office was still going. It was very run down when the Richters took over. After fighting sinking wood floats for 15 years, Bob and Nancy bought a section of the Hood Canal floating bridge and had it towed north as a platform for the store. Billy did the move, pulling up both the store and freight shed onto the huge cement structure. Echo Bay is the only local resort which stays open year-round, running a post office, small general store and a gas dock. All the other once-thriving communities of Sullivan Bay and Minstrel Island close all winter. Bob and Nancy's decision to stay open has helped the community stay alive.

Pat and Fraser arrived with two children and two boats. *New Fraser*, which they were living on, sank with all their belongings while they were in Port McNeill getting supplies. The community scooped everything out of the water, and washed and dried it all, from clothes to photographs. Billy pulled the poor old boat ashore and dragged its engine out with his D4 Cat. Somehow, the family survived two years on Pat's little 35-foot *Ellerton Cove*, until they were able to renovate a floathouse and move in.

For me the most important new arrival rounded the corner into the bay in a 1926 tugboat, *Gabriola*. Eric Nelson had been up this way several times before, from Sechelt, and when it became clear that Sechelt was changing from a small community to a suburb, he thought more seriously about the Broughton Archipelago. A log salvager, he called me one day on the VHF and asked if he could tie his logs to my float for the night. There are no private conversations on the VHF radio and my neighbours ribbed me plenty later — "What a line!" A few months later, my dock became Eric's home port.

Billy figures seaplanes caused a big change in remote communities. "They allow people to work here without living here." As I too watch people drain away, it reminds me of a hot-air balloon ride I took. When I got into the basket, I was asked not to get out suddenly, because without my weight the balloon

Schoolchildren and teacher out with dolphins. (PHOTO BY ALEXANDRA MORTON)

The Echo Bay School student body in 1989. (PHOTO BY ALEXANDRA MORTON)

would drift away. Echo Bay is the same. If the school loses one more child it might close, more families would leave and then the post office would close, and so on. We lobbied the school board to extend the school, to include grades eight, nine, and ten, and to use our remote school as a field-trip destination for children in the cities. They let us try both, but neither really worked and then in 1992 the situation began to turn around. Three families moved back and a couple more have arrived since then.

A community as small as Echo Bay is deeply satisfying to live in. While the social responsibility can be taxing, the children thrive. I remember not wanting to attend a square dance, shortly after Robin drowned, but I went, because they couldn't complete the square without me. When the children try to raise money for field trips you have to go to the bingo game. If you haven't seen someone in too long, you go check on them, no matter whether you wanted to go out that day or not. During a storm everyone keeps an eye out for someone. Though friction, arguments and feuds all abound, this is the way people were meant to live, in close-knit, co-operative communities.

While Billy was born in the Mainland, many people came to the area for a variety of reasons: some to make their fortunes, others to seek adventure and a few to find escape. Though there are many excellent sites to build homesteads, some people chose the most formidable spots to live, and the only reason they survived was that the Mainland community helped.

Pete Johnson came to Tribune Channel in about 1920 from Texas. He was a big man, strong as a bull, and he wore a big cowboy hat.

Pete Johnson came on the steamboat with only his pack on his back and $100 to his name. He got a job in one of the camps and in a while bought a good rowboat. On weekends he would go up Tribune to look for a good claim, but he really didn't know what he was looking for. There were some handloggers out there already, so he looked at what they were doing and soon he found a claim that looked good to him. He asked one of the other handloggers about it and he said it was a good claim. But it was a bad spot for wind and tide; that was why no one else had taken it.

Pete got the claim, quit his job and found a flat spot where he built a little shack out of split cedar. Then he started to log. He found there was lots to learn, but as time went by he found he could get bigger trees down to the water easier than small ones. So he just picked the big ones and got a good reputation for putting real good booms together.

When he was fed up with his rowboat, he started to build a bigger boat. He found a nice big yellow cedar, split long boards and planed them smooth. He did a nice job and it was a good boat for that time, 26 feet long and flat bottomed. He put a four hp Easthope in it. Now he was set; he could tow his logs in a lot faster. He logged that claim for 15 years, then found another one, but it was too far from his shack. So he built a new one on a float that he could move.

He moved it to a windy little bay, hung on for a few years, then moved to Wahkana Bay for a few years, then Kwatsi Bay for a time, then Thompson Sound. He handlogged all over Tribune. I have found where he went 3,000 feet up the sidehill and ran big firs and spruce down to the water. You could always tell old Pete's stumps; the springboard hole was so far down from where he cut, because he was so tall. I found one place where he had run a real big fir down and it had gotten stuck in a rocky canyon, a bad place to work, but he had chopped through four feet of fir with an axe. Some job.

Everyone liked Pete. I never heard anyone ever say anything bad about him. His little white floathouse was so small and always neat and clean. He logged till he was over 70 years old and when he retired, he tied to a logging camp. He would watch camp for them and do odd jobs, and they took care of him and let him eat in the cookhouse. That camp was owned by Fred and Babs Buzzard who were old-timers from Thompson Sound. Fred had been around for a long time and when they moved into Shoal Harbour in 1966, they took old Pete with them. He put his old boat on the beach in Thompson Sound before he left. He hated to part with it, but it was getting old and in bad shape. Well, he lived in Shoal Harbour till he passed away when he was 93.

He had a good long life and he loved Tribune Channel just like I do. I don't think there is a more beautiful place. Well, Fred and Babs kept his little house for a few years and then sold it to a young couple just moving out to the Mainland, George and Susie Jahn. They lived in it for a few years and then sold it to Jim O'Donnell. He sold it to an old trapper. After he died it was sold to Dennis Richards, and it burned in 1993. So that was the end of a little house that was built in Tribune Channel.

Frank Benjamin came to Tribune Channel in 1910, when he was 18. Some said he was a remittance man, paid to stay out of England to end the embarrassment of a wealthy family. Frank heard there was a lot of money to be made handlogging, so he got a claim and all the tools: a cross-cut saw, an axe, two Gilchrist jacks, a springboard, a rowboat and a boom auger.

A springboard is a piece of two-by-six board about five feet long. It is pointed at one end and has a metal plate bolted on top to stick into the tree. A notch is cut in the tree, the springboard is jammed into the notch and it makes a platform above the flare of the tree's roots for the logger to stand on. Sometimes they had to go up two or three times to get away from the swell of a big butt.

Frank built a little shack on a float and lived in Wahkana Bay, but he didn't like it there, because it was a long way to tow his logs home each night with his rowboat. He looked around for some land and settled on Irving Point. He bought 165 acres for 25¢ an acre. Irving Point is on the dark side of Tribune Channel with virtually no shelter for a boat nor any sunlight, but he had a beautiful view of Bond Sound and the mountains, and in 1912 he built a little shack down by the water and painted it green.

In spring he started to clear land for a garden and soon he planted spuds. He loved potatoes and ate them regularly with the deer he shot and canned each fall. When he wasn't working on his homestead he was logging, or picking up the logs that escaped from other loggers and drifted by. There were a lot of logs drifting around before people started bundling them up with cables and he was in a good spot to see them floating by. He rowed ten miles to Simoom Sound for his mail and supplies.

Frank didn't like rowing so he bought a gas boat with a three hp Fairbanks Morse engine. At first he was happy with his powerful new boat, because he could tow his logs much faster and didn't have to row. He tried fishing, and rigged the little boat for trolling, but caught too few fish to make it worth the trip to Simoom Sound to sell them.

So he gave up on fishing, cleared a little more land and bought chickens. When the First World War started, six men hid out on the west side of Bond Sound. Familiar with being an exile, Frank supplied them with food and whatever else they needed. He had a good radio and he kept them informed about what was going on in the world. He loved reading and many of his books were about radios and steam engines.

After a few years he wanted a bigger boat, so he got a 24-footer with a four hp Easthope gas engine. This boat wasn't much bigger, but it had a cabin, bunk and little woodstove called a "Trout." There were two kinds of little woodstoves, the Trout and the Cod;

most boats had the Trout because it was larger. When Frank wanted more power, he replaced the Easthope with a two cycle, ten hp Anderson and rigged the boat for trolling again. He didn't do any better than before and so gave up a second time.

He had constant problems anchoring his boats because of where he lived; there was no shelter from the wind or swell. Then a winter storm came down the channel and broke his boat loose. It went ashore and by morning was beyond repair, so he was back to the rowboat. Bob Lawson and his dad had a small boat with no engine that they didn't use. They gave it to Frank and he put the old Anderson in her.

When Frank decided he wanted a bigger garden he bought a small tractor. With the tractor he could also pull bigger logs, farther from the water, so he was doing well logging his land. Frank had an old telescope and whenever a boat went by he cracked open the door, checked the boat with the telescope and wrote down the name, how many people were in it and how fast it was going. He liked a shot of rum at the end of the day, and always smoked Ogden cigarettes, which he called "Uptowners."

One night the new boat went on the beach too and that was the end of it, so he bought a little steel, 26-foot lifeboat and put a Star gas engine in it. Now he had lots of power, but in a few years the boat was rusted so badly it leaked terribly and he put it on the beach, by his house, where the remains of it can still be seen.

A big logging camp moved in nearby so Frank began relying on them for supplies; the Union Steamship stopped at the camp so he had access to pretty much anything he needed. He made a deal with the camp, letting them log more of his land, and made lots of money. He bought *Western Swell*, a 34-foot troller, determined once again to become a fisherman, but he still couldn't catch fish.

Frank left as an old man to live with a sister in Nova Scotia but his little green shack is still standing in the shadows of Irving Point. Years after Frank left, Billy found his detailed records on all the boats which had passed and the stacks of books on radios and steam engines. Jae had once offered Frank magazines to read, but he had rejected them, saying, "I'm a scientific man and I only read scientific books."

Every time Billy passes the house he remembers the door cracking open and the telescope peering out. "When I go ashore I always wonder why he picked such a place to build, when there were so many good places in those days and so easy to get. But I don't think anyone will ever understand why some people do odd things."

Frank Benjamin's old house. (PHOTO BY ALEXANDRA MORTON)

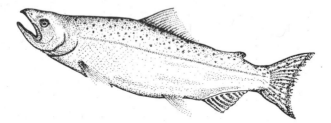

CHAPTER TEN

It may well be later than we think, but it's not too late.

Terry Glavin, *Dead Reckoning*, 1996

IN 1995, BILLY was invited to sit on the Mount Waddington Community Resource Board. Meeting every second Monday in Port McNeill, this board was called together to "provide local input and advice on provincial decisions which directly affect the resource base within the Board area." The board area includes from the Broughton Archipelago north to Cape Caution, and the Port McNeill and Port Hardy areas. Billy was asked to represent Area "A," his beloved Mainland. Among the other resources represented are logging, mining and tourism.

Sitting on a board was awkward at first. There were motions, votes and proposals, and it was a more formal gathering than Billy had ever experienced. It was also a big commitment of time. While most members jump in their cars and drive for a few minutes, or up to half an hour, it is a six-hour round trip for Billy. Often he comes back the same day, arriving home at one in the morning. But he was honoured to be asked and he looked forward to representing the area he loved. It definitely needed help and he felt he had some good ideas on what needed to be done.

Wild salmon require a wide variety of functioning habitat, from mountain streams to the international waters of the open Pacific. Oil drillers, fish farmers, loggers, miners and developers all want to use salmon habitat. Unfortunately, none of them have demonstrated that they can or are willing to share habitat with salmon. To date they have only killed the fish with their practices. Billy found himself arguing on behalf of the salmon among the richest sectors in the region. While this was enormously frustrating, it honed his diplomatic skills. The other members of the board do not always want to hear what Billy has to say, but they respect his honesty and wisdom.

In 1996, the province asked Billy to sit on an Environmental Review Board examining the impact of salmon farming and he said yes. Having been drawn into this issue as well, I attended the meetings as a member of the public. At those meetings I watched an amazing transformation. Billy has no tolerance for lies and less for anything destroying the coast, so the steam pouring from his ears was nearly visible as he sat and listened.

At the first few meetings this shy man slammed his fist on the table and his voice quivered with rage. But by mid-winter he was laying out the truth in his plain-spoken, good-natured way. The room stilled when Billy spoke and I felt great pride to know him. The truth is the truth, but when the spokesman is a storyteller in the old tradition, everyone *knows* it is the truth. The boy in Freshwater Bay would have stood tall to know he would be this man.

By spring Proctor was bent over charts with the premier of the province, Glen Clark, explaining the mysteries of the salmon and negotiating for their survival. Scientists say we are at a crossroads. We have five years to turn around the declines. Billy has become increasingly frustrated at people's acceptance that wild salmon are dying out. At salmon-farm meetings he was told he must accept that wild salmon are a thing of the past. He expected the farmers to take that stand, because the wild salmon compete on the market with farm fish, but when he heard it on the docks in Port Hardy, among the commercial fleet, he realized that the fish will die if the fishermen give up.

It's pretty sad, when you think about it, what this country used to be like. I've seen a bit of it, but before I was born even, Jesus, it must have been really phenomenal around here for fish. Canneries booming away in Knight Inlet, Kingcome, Alert Bay, Bones Bay. Kingcome used to have a run of a couple of million pinks, and 20,000 chinook. Christ, now it's got nothing, 68 fish.

If we're going to bring the fish back, number one we've got to do lots of habitat work. They've proved that down in southern California. The trollers down there caught 850,000 chinooks; that's up from almost nothing in the 1980s. That shows you what can be done.

Billy with Premier Glen Clark at a meeting about salmon farms, June 1997. (PHOTO BY ALEXANDRA MORTON)

On the central coast up around Bella Bella there are 65 watersheds that have never been touched by loggers and the fishing there is still good.

A Plan to Help Save Our Wild Pacific Salmon

I have been a commercial fisher for 54 years. My father was a fisher, who started with a skiff in 1928. My daughter deckhanded for me and now my grandsons are fishing with me. Over the last 20 years there have been many plans and reports and buybacks with the latest being the Mifflin Plan. Except for the Cruickshank report, all these plans and reports have one thing in common: they were written by people not familiar with the industry.

For the last 15 years our Fisheries ministers have had a life cycle shorter than a pink salmon. There has been no continuity, and a lot of their advisers don't know much about the coast and fishing as a way of life. Here are my recommendations on how to help our wild Pacific salmon.

The Seine Fleet

I don't think there is much more to change in this user group except to improve on the releasing of non-targeted species and make it mandatory to drum in more slowly when by-catch or grilse are a concern.

The Gillnet Fleet

Not much else that can be done in this sector.

The Troll Fleet

Make it mandatory to use barbless or crimped barb hooks when fishing for spring salmon. This will make it easier to release non-targeted species. Use only four lines when fishing spring salmon, because with six lines, by the time the fisherman gets to the last line (usually the back pig), the fish is drowned or too weak to survive. Most of the time you can catch just as many fish with four lines.

The Sport-Fishing Sector

We have got to get the *sport* back into sport fishing. The way it is now, it is just trophy fishing. No sport fishing allowed in rivers and streams until such time as there are enough fish to warrant having an in-river sport fishery.

Set an annual limit of 20 coho.

Ban triple hooks coastwide.

No more catch-and-release on the inside waters for coho and springs, because when the fish are nearing their rivers, heavy with spawn, they cannot stand the stress of being hooked and "played."

Department of Fisheries and Oceans

There are many things DFO must do to save our chinook and coho stocks. There has to be more habitat work to restore the spawning grounds. There has to be much more enforcement in the sport sector. Without it, DFO has no idea how many coho and chinook are being caught by sport fishers. More exact tallies are essential. DFO has got to stop turning a blind eye to the sport sector.

There should be sport boundaries on every river and stream just like the commercial boundaries.

DFO should stop using helicopters to fly over rivers to count fish. The process of spawning is disrupted when a helicopter flies over and startles the fish. If a female has just laid her eggs and the male is scared away by the helicopter while in the process of fertilizing them, the eggs will not be fertile; they will die. I have been in helicopters counting fish and I am quite certain this abandonment of redds is a common occurrence in some of our rivers and streams.

We have to ban the use of pesticides in *all* our watersheds along the coast, regardless of what some experts tell us, because they have been wrong in the past and we can't let them experiment on every generation of fish.

Reduce, or stop altogether, the use of electroshockers. I am sure they are unnecessary and detrimental to both fry and broodstock. [Electroshocking is a barbaric method of counting salmon in a river. An electric probe is stuck in the water and a shock administered. This stuns the fish and they float to the surface. It is easy for the counter, but hard on the fish, breaking the backs of adults. Studies show it reduces the young salmon's ability to survive, but it is still a popular method of counting fry.]

Blasting for road building close to salmon-spawning habitat should only be done when there are no salmon eggs present. When a sharp blast is set off close to salmon redds, the shock can kill the eggs up to at least 300 metres away. I know this because it happened in our hatchery at Scott Cove twice in the last ten years. Both times, a blast from the log dump over 200 metres from the hatchery killed eggs in the hatchery.

DFO also needs advisers who understand how fishers think and can look at some of the problems from a fisher's point of view, not some economist sitting in front of a computer giving advice. Computer models are not the way things are out on the grounds.

DFO has got to have the authority to issue spot closures for the sport-fishing sector. The way it is now, it can take up to ten days and that is too long; the fish are all caught. We all know they can issue closures in the blink of an eye to the commercial sector.

Sport-fishing lodges should have to purchase a licence just like commercial fishers. Each sport fisher should be issued a punch card with their licence and when this card is full and they have caught their limit, that's it for the year. This could be accomplished by hiring students for each lodge and that person's job would be to check each fisher as they come in and punch their card.

There should be a moratorium on the number of lodges along the coast till such time as the salmon stocks are built up to warrant the expansion. Charter boats have got to be monitored more closely. Because of their mobility, they can move into some inlet that should not be fished at all.

We commercial fishers have got to fight for the fish or we are going to lose big time. We have to stop blaming the other person, because even if you only take one fish, you are part of the problem.

If we lose the wild Pacific salmon, we not only lose our livelihood, we lose many other species that feed on salmon, all the way from the North Pacific to the mountain tops all along the coast. We have got to remember that salmon are a fast renewable resource.

I hope this report gets to a lot of people and they take the time to read and think about some of the statements I have made. I know some won't like what I have said, but before you get too upset just think for a minute. I truly believe that if these simple recommendations were put into effect, we would have a future to give our *children*.

★★★

If you start in San Francisco and travel north, you will find that every watershed has been logged until you reach Bond Sound in Tribune Channel. Grizzlies still inhabit Bond Sound and salmon spawn through every inch of gravel. The tiny water ouzel bobs along the shore and runs underwater on the bottom of the creek, hunting in a manner unique among birds. Swans, geese and ducks circle the tawny grass delta in the fall and wolf howls echo across the sound. Bond Sound is slated to be logged within the next five years, part of the rich delta bulldozed into a log-sorting ground.

Billy makes a point of visiting his neighbours regularly and when his speedboat pulls up to the beach we put the kettle on for tea. Usually, he ties up his boat carefully and makes his way up to the house slowly, looking at the garden, talking to the dogs. But last spring he leaped out of the boat, threw the bow line at a rock and was at the door an instant later.

"They're going to log Bond Sound and I'm going stop them if I have to stand there with my gun!"

"*Wow*, come in, Billy! What's this all about?"

They can't have every single watershed. It isn't right.

Something's got to be left for the future. There are three salmon streams in the sound, and one of them has all five species of salmon, plus steelhead, cutthroat and Dolly Varden trout. Almost all of the watershed is undisturbed, 2,000-year-old forest. Bond Sound is prime grizzly bear habitat that needs to be protected. There are also black bear, deer, mountain goats, mink, marmot, pikas, marten, raccoon, otter, beaver, wolverine, porcupine, fisher and weasels. There are several species of hawks and owls and a vast number of songbirds nesting in the area. Canada geese and several species of ducks nest and winter in Bond Sound.

Trumpeter swans winter in the lowland lakes and golden eagles are often seen in the mountains. There is also critical wildlife wintering range and a rest stop for migrating water fowl. There are several small, crystal-clear streams in the sound and some are glacier fed. Six alpine lakes feed the streams, and vast alpine meadows grow heather and many species of wildflowers.

Then Billy asked, "How do you save a watershed anyway?" I didn't know.

Billy didn't go fishing that year. He went up to Bond Sound, cut a trail and started taking people in to see the wonder. A group of fishermen from Sointula got funding to pull a natural log jam out of the creek and when I visited, it was a sight to give a person hope. As the ripe huckleberries twinkled and blinked from the shore, burly seine fishermen were rallied around the survival of one of the last thriving salmon-birthing grounds.

Bond Sound. (PHOTO BY ALEXANDRA MORTON)

Billy took his quest to save this piece of our world to the Mount Waddington Community Resource Board. He also asked the board to make the Mainland a "pesticide-free zone." Surprisingly, they voted unanimously to draft a letter to the Ministry of Environment. But they never sent the letter. Instead, the board, with strong logging membership, took another vote *not* to send the letter.

The Ministry of Environment granted Interfor, a large logging company, a permit to spray the Kakweikan watershed above Thompson Sound with herbicides. The community of Echo Bay rallied and decided to appeal the permit. Already the Clear, Satsalla, Atlatzi and LakLah had been sprayed in 1997 with chemicals documented as being highly toxic to cold-water fish such as salmon and trout, and the salmon in those rivers were dying. Throughout the Mainland, in Wakeman, Kingcome and Mackenzie, the sudden drop in salmon returning to those rivers exactly matched the date they were sprayed with pesticides.

Sierra Legal Defence agreed to represent members of the community in our appeal against the pesticide permit while the hatchery was represented by Kate Pinsonneault. When the lawyers and community members viewed the watershed, we found it laced with streams. Despite assurances from government and industry that no "substantial" amounts of the toxic chemicals would reach the river, no one could see how that could possibly be true with so much water running through the cut block. We also found that in many of the treatment blocks, the brush Interfor intended to kill wasn't present. Why were they even thinking of spraying?

While the appeal board ruled that Interfor had misrepresented the number of creeks, and that the chemical was toxic to fish, and accused the Ministry of Environment of a "cavalier attitude" toward the protection of coho habiatat, the spraying was allowed. The plan is to spray in August, just as the salmon enter their rivers to spawn. They intend to spray an area smaller than they had first planned, due to our appeal, but we didn't succeed in having the permit revoked, which would have allowed only manual brush clearing.

Billy can't sleep nights. His living-room bookshelf has become crowded with books on the state of our planet. *Our Stolen Future* by Theo Colborn haunts him as he watches his grandsons fish and argue just beyond the bay in their little rowboat. He bought copies of the book and sent them to the Ministry of Environment bureaucrat who granted the pesticide permits, thus taking life on this planet one step closer to a painful, grotesque death.

No environmental battle is ever won. The corporate foothold on Earth is so big they barely notice what obstacles any one person can throw before them. But each fall that a salmon spawns is a victory. Gradually, if more people realize the power of the individual, we will turn the course of our species from certain death to co-existence with life.

★★★

Holly Tracy of Sointula asked me to shoot a video of Bond Sound in the on-going effort to preserve that watershed. I asked Billy if he would go with me, because I didn't want to face a grizzly bear alone. Billy laughed at me, as usual. In 40 years he'd only seen three grizzlies there. But he is always willing to walk the pristine valley.

With cameras draped around my neck and shoulders we set off from the beach. Our feet sank deep in the loamy soil; goose pellets were everywhere. The sedge grass, combed by the wind, spread around us in patterns as ancient as life itself. Geese wheeled and honked above. As we entered the forest, it grew dim and we stopped to watch the water ouzel dance. Chum salmon heads stared up at us from the path, part of the rich Pacific food chain, nutrients draining out of their flesh to feed the soil and river. On a stretch of sand on the far side of the creek, fresh bear tracks followed the water's edge.

I stopped frequently to film, but I wanted to keep up with Billy. I had no idea what I'd do if a bear got between us. Then I heard Billy say softly, "There's one."

I figured he meant a salmon that hadn't spawned yet. I jumped down onto the sand bar and with a jolt of recognition saw the grizzly. The bear was looking for salmon, swaying as his long legs carried him in an unmistakable saunter. While I filmed, my pounding heartbeat was recorded as well. We didn't move until the bear was gone, vanished into the gloom of his forest home. Then we turned and left to fight for his life.

Epilogue

Billy Proctor was born in a time when there was a bounty on every predator. No tolerance was granted towards any species which dared compete with us. Humans have fought tenaciously to make a place for ourselves throughout the world's phenomenally diverse environments. With extraordinary resourcefulness, we grasp every advantage, redesign habitats to make them our own and ruthlessly dominate competitors. As a result, we have thrived. But now, as we stand firmly atop the pyramid of life and continue to grind forward blindly, we are destroying what holds us aloft.

Most people sense change is taking place. Deep within, our instincts sense the balance is shifting. With nothing left to conquer, we are now killing ourselves, our children and the other species to which we are still inexorably linked. Our truly remarkable minds create whatever we can imagine: materials, objects and environments which never existed before we thought of them.

However, we deny reality just as effectively as we create it, and therein lies the danger.

When a species becomes so successful that it destroys its environment, natural forces kick in to contain it. Over-population leads to starvation, disease and violent behaviour. Most species, unable to recognize impending doom, succumb to these crushing forces. We are perched at the edge of this precipice, facing the ultimate test of our extraordinary intelligence. Can we alter, in an evolutionary instant, the wildly successful survival strategies which have carried us to this pinnacle? Can we respond with unprecedented speed and purpose?

If we wait too long, we simply won't survive. Nature is ruthless.

I ignored the degradation of this planet successfully for years. I just wanted to study whales and I tried not to think about their welfare, their habitat or their prospects for long-term survival, because it was too disturbing. I had blinders firmly clamped in place, but Billy kept coming around with his plain-spoken observations and I was forced to look around. He has a way of making it all so clear, so simple, so unavoidable. Dedicated as they are, city-born environmentalists don't have the impact of one who is wearing logging boots.

Billy Proctor has had the courage to look at his life, examine his own impact on his beloved Mainland and make changes. His example has affected the people around him profoundly.

When Billy was a boy, shooting everything was normal, and creeks were the best way to get logs down to the sea. Catching as many fish and falling as many trees as he could was the goal. Making as much money as possible, doing what he liked was his life. He became a highliner fisherman, a handlogger with one of the biggest wood quotas on the coast and a good trapper, and he and his family built the largest homestead for miles around.

People shrug and say, "What can I do? How can I possibly make a difference? One person can't change everything." Well, that is true, but the fact is each of us *does* know where we could make a change for the better, if we wanted to.

Billy has taken that step. Made less money, done things he'd rather not, things which terrified him, but he accepted responsibility for his life. And it is impossible to ignore that. He has started a ripple in his corner of the world which his neighbours, friends, and acquaintances have felt and to which they have been compelled to contribute.

Billy brought me a salmon one day a couple of years ago. He loves fishing for spring salmon in winter when they are feeding in the Mainland. Their flesh is so rich with oils, so sweet, that you can't eat a whole lot of it at once. Some of these "winter springs," as they are called, get quite big, and if it's more than he and Yvonne can eat, Billy makes the rounds, giving the neighbours a piece.

When he got to my place he handed me a fish and said, "Don't you laugh now, but the Natives say that if you want to keep salmon coming back, you gotta fillet them right away and put the head and backbone back in ocean. As you let go of the bones you have got to say 'thank you.' "

I did as instructed and watched thoughtfully as he roared away. Billy was giving his quest to preserve salmon every level of himself, from the physical work in the creeks, to the mental work of studying to prepare for meetings, to the spiritual out on the water. No stones left unturned.

The power of one is all we have, but we all have it.

More Nautical Narratives from TouchWood Editions

ISBN 1-894898-07-9
$44.95

ISBN 1-894898-12-5
$17.95

ISBN 0-920663-60-5
$24.95

ISBN 0-920663-70-2
$16.95

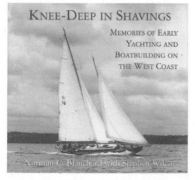

ISBN 0-920663-63-X
$34.95

ISBN 0-920663-01-X
$12.95

May be purchased from quality booksellers or e-mail
greatbooks@heritagehouse.ca for information on availability.

Alexandra Morton is a whale researcher, biologist, photographer and writer. She graduated from the American University in Washington, D.C., in 1978, and since then she has studied dolphins and orcas in California and British Columbia. In 1984, she and her filmmaker husband, Robin Morton, moved to Echo Bay on Gilford Island. Robin drowned in 1986, but Alexandra stayed in the little community with their son, Jarret, and carried on with her research.

Alexandra, internationally known as "The Whale Lady," is familiar to thousands of people through her TV appearances, films and slide shows, and her books *Siwiti — A Whale's Story* and *In the Company of Whales*. A documentary film about her and her work, called *Alexandra's Echo*, was released in 2003.